THE STERLING BOOK OF
RAMANA MAHARSHI

Other Books in this Series

Indian Classical Dances
SHOVANA NARAYAN

Buddha and His Teachings
KINGSLEY HEENDENIYA

Ma Sarada: The Miracle of Love
M. SIVARAMKRISHNA

Bhagvad Gita
O. P. GHAI

Hinduism
DR KARAN SINGH

THE STERLING BOOK OF
RAMANA MAHARSHI

Prof. M. Sivaramkrishna

Sterling Paperbacks

STERLING PAPERBACKS
An imprint of
Sterling Publishers (P) Ltd.
A-59, Okhla Industrial Area, Phase-II,
New Delhi-110020.
Tel: 26387070, 26386209; Fax: 91-11-26383788
E-mail: sterlingpublishers@airtelbroadband.in
ghai@nde.vsnl.net.in
www.sterlingpublishers.com

The Sterling Book of: Ramana Maharshi
© 2008, Prof. M. Sivaramkrishna
ISBN 978-81-207-9451-1

All rights are reserved.
No part of this publication may be reproduced, stored in a retrieval system or transmitted, in any form or by any means, mechanical, photocopying, recording or otherwise, without prior written permission of the original publisher.

Printed and Published by Sterling Publishers Pvt. Ltd.,
New Delhi-110 020.

Contents

	Preface	7
	Introduction	9
1.	No Difference	15
2.	Witness The Passing Show: It's *Cinemaya*	20
3.	The Mason's Prayer	27
4.	"The Body Is Mortal: Why Feel Sad? I Am With You!"	33
5.	Where Is Our Own Pencil?	39
6.	Everything Is Alive, Pulsing With Life	44
7.	Be God Yourself!	50
8.	Turn Your Life Over To That	58
9.	Bhagawan In Czechoslovakia	63
10.	The One Who Tried But Couldn't Get Away!	68
11.	Where Is The 'I' To Identify A Name?	75
12.	To Be Angry Or Not? That's The Question	82

13.	Peace Of Bliss	89
14.	You Also Don't Take	95
15.	When 'I' Enters, Bhagawan Exits	99
16.	Cover The Curry, Put The Lid On The Mind	106
17.	"I Will Sit On The Rock Brushing My Teeth!"	111
18.	Bhagawan: The Master Storyteller	115

Preface

This is not a biography of Bhagawan Ramana. Quite a few biographies exist such as the ones by B. V. Narasimha Swamy and Arthur Osborne. Instead, I have focused on incidents which reveal the practical aspects of Bhagawan Ramana's basic spiritual outlook: how he responded to human contexts which are not separate from the so-called spiritual quest.

Literature on Bhagawan Ramana is very vast. I selected only a few aspects which I hope will be of interest to readers. The day-to-day life of Bhagawan seemed to me much more interesting than abstract ideas. This does not mean that he was an abstract thinker. I wanted to highlight the fact that Bhagawan Ramana followed the *natural* way of self-enquiry. Every incident in this sense becomes an illuminator of the path to peace and joyful living. Bhagawan was humane and it is this aspect that is reflected in his life and message.

I have drawn from Ramanashram Publications for the content. But I have not reproduced anything verbatim. I thank the authorities of the Ashram.

Finally, this book was possible only because of what I learnt from 'Sri Ram' my anonymous mentor. Mere thanks are not enough for him.

Dr. Sumita Roy was of immense help in the final shaping of the book. I thank her for her involvement in the preparation of the book.

Mrs. Prabha did the DTP work with care and dedication. My thanks to her.

I thank Mr. S.K. Ghai for accepting this for publication.

M. SIVARAMKRISHNA

Introduction

The celebrated psychologist C. G. Jung observed that "what we find in the life and teachings of Ramana Maharshi is the purest of India; with its breath of world-liberated and liberating humanity, it is a chant of millenniums." In a similar vein, the doyen of contemporary consciousness studies, Ken Wilber, describing India as "one of the most astonishing and profound geographical sources of spiritual awareness on the planet," says that if he were stranded on a desert island and had to take a book with him, "*Talks with Ramana Maharshi* is of its two or three I always mention."

150 years after his advent, Ramana Maharshi is today in the heart and consciousness of almost every seeker as a perennial inspiration. Like the sacred Arunachala Mountain in Tiruvannamalai, he shines with singular splendour. Serene, unruffled, rock-like in the steadiness of an eternal Truth, he embodied a Presence that communes without language and a peace that percolates to the depths of one's being, illumining its interior in the most *natural* way. *Natural* because experiences came to him before they were confirmed by books and scholars!

The most crucial experience came when he was 17 years old. Born on 29 December 1879 (Ramakrishna was still alive), in Tiruchuli, Tamilnadu, he was named Venkataraman. A good athletic frame, gregarious by temperament, loving and lovable there was, nevertheless, nothing to set him apart from the other boys. Perhaps, the exterior was a facade. For deep down, there was a luminous spark which needed the right kind of ignition to blaze forth as the radiant breath of the Eternal.

Then came the remarkable experience. He was in robust health and nothing prefaced the event. On that day, he later recalled, he "sat alone" in a room on the first floor when "a sudden and unmistakable fear of death seized me. I felt I was going to die." For this feeling nothing was there in the body as a warrant. He knew there was no physical basis for the fear.

Venkataraman did something unique. Disregarding the paralysing fear, and the thought of rushing for help never struck him, he started enquiring into the nature of the reality of this fear. The 17-year-old imitated "a corpse to lend the air of reality" and visualised everything that happens thereafter: the corpse, the consigning to flames, the residue of nothing but ash. "With this death of the body," he asked himself "am 'I' dead? Is the body 'I'? The body is silent and inert. But 'I' feel the full force of my personality and even the sound of 'I' within myself – apart from the body. So I am a spirit transcending the body. The material body dies, but the spirit transcending it cannot be touched by Death." And the profound Truth dawned (never to set at any dusk), "I am therefore the deathless spirit."

The transcendence of the fear of *marana*, death, unfolded in the Presence of Ramana, the radiant Face of Eternity. And, he declared, later, the *vichara* rooted in and roving around 'I' was not intellectual gymnastics, or a sterile, stoic indifference and detachment; it was unique in a sense. The Buddha saw a corpse, Paramahamsa Ramakrishna seized a sword to kill himself defiantly at the denial, apparently, of Mother Kali to reveal Herself. Maharshi registered the experience of death on his body and consciousness and came back to report that the presence of Death is not, as Shakespeare would have it, "the unseen land from which no traveller returns." On the contrary, death is not 'the *end* but a *bend*,' a door to eternality. The existentialist's despair of 'no exit' is a mental construct.

The mystic poet Kabir put it tersely, "Death after death the world dies/but no one knows how to die/the servant Kabir died such a death/as he won't have to die again." And this is precisely what Ramana Maharshi did.

He heard now the insistent call of Arunachala Shiva – the very word sent horripilations all over the body, left everything behind, heeded the call and reached Tiruvannamalai. He remained for the rest of his 'life' there – an achalam. Unmoving but moving imperceptibly the minds and hearts of countless seekers, who thronged to the mountain and later to the ashram; Paul Brunton, Arthur Osborne, S. S.Cohen, Major Chadwick and above all the renowned Kavyakantha Ganapati Muni who declared him as 'Bhagawan Ramana,' Annamalai Swami, Muruganar, the renowned Telugu writer G. Venkatachalam and so many others.

They all found *naturalness* as the most outstanding feature of Bhagawan. Natural because it is linked to what everyone of us experiences, the need to even exist, the sense of 'I'. Hence Maharshi's classic path, enquiry into "who am I?" Am I the 'I' swayed by emotions, buffeted by the vicissitudes of life, goes to sleep, to dream and per chance to die? But, alongside, there are also sporadic moments of peace and tranquillity, perhaps, in deep sleep. Are we then sleep-walkers deriving our sense of identity from a fickle and fluctuating 'I' and therefore going through 'life's fitful fever'? This 'I' which afraid of final dissolution realises, as sage J.Krishnamurthi said, "only at the point of death that it had not lived at all?" Is life merely "what sex sows and death reaps?"

"All living beings," said Bhagawan, "desire to be happy always, without misery." And "to gain that *happiness which is our nature* and which is experienced in the state of deep sleep where there is no mind, one should know one's self. For that the path of knowledge, the enquiry of 'who am I' is the principal means."

With cognitive models and paradigms clamouring around us like cackling geese, the experience of self, as containing but not conditioned by the 'I', is a corrective; it is, in that sense, natural. And, secondly, it is so simple and dispenses with (though it does not discredit) rituals. Maharshi, as far as we know, never seems to have 'initiated' anyone. He treated all as equals but as Swami Ranganathananda put it, we all think he is unique and superior. Like Dakshinamurti, the symbol of vibrant silence, Bhagawan is a PRESENCE AND A POWER. For, this loincloth-clad one, *kaupinadhari,* is a *Kaivalyavihari*: one who roamed in the vast, limitless stretches of the Cosmic Consciousness that encompasses everything.

Literally everything is integral, interrelated, interdependent. The zen truth, "from the mountain to the market place" finds a glorious exemplar in Maharshi. This is his third aspect. Every activity got integrated into the orchestra of his amazingly ordinary but effulgent, joyful 'lifestyle'. Pounding rice, cutting vegetables, preparing *idli*, concocting from, often recycled vegetable peeling, ravishingly delicious *chutneys*, or simply sitting in vibrant silence on a gloriously uncomfortable stone-bench; there was only the loving and lovable presence. The One who enacted, neither acted or reacted.

From this integrality comes what we pontificate as ecological oneness. The cow Lakshmi, the monkeys that thronged, the birds that settled on his shoulder, even the serpents, tigers – all were *his family*. He even nursed an egg, trampled upon or hit back, to its *natural* process of coming out of the shell!

And, finally for us, the harrowing scene of the body's decay by cancer. Even to imagine the pain is an ordeal. But to the end he was rooted in the experience of the fact that he registered on his body at 17 years that there is no death. How then can one grieve? He designed the whole scene, so it seems, to *show* not merely *tell*, its truth of life beyond death. The incredible imperviousness to the body gloriously proclaims, the much ignored fact, that life linked to its ending is in time. Ramana Bhagawan represents the timeless – encompassing the whole of the cosmos in his love. Eventually, it is Maharshi's love that passeth understanding and therefore frees us from the polarities that understanding inevitably engenders. The shooting star that appeared in the sky when he left his body has fallen gently in our hearts. That is the experience we should nourish and nurture on his 150th 'Birthday'.

He beckons to us, "the whitest spot in a white space," not just for India, as Jung said, "but now for everyone, anyone who would like to enquire, Who am I?"

1

No Difference

When someone asked the celebrated sage, Swami Ranganathananda, what is the uniqueness of Bhagawan Ramana, he said: "He says that, 'there is absolutely no difference between you and me'. But we say, 'Maharshi, you are different! We are ordinary, you are extraordinary!' The uniqueness of Bhagawan is to deny anything special about himself. In fact, no sage attributes uniqueness to himself (or herself).

But, like all other saints and sages, Ramana Bhagawan was fond of seizing an ordinary incident to strike home such truths. He looks beyond the ordinary to show an extraordinary truth. But, paradoxically, only to point out that what appears extraordinary is simply the overlooked, misperceived truth in the ordinary. And quite often, equally paradoxically, the truth is suggested, even shown to staunch devotees.

The year was 1939, but do time, date and calendar matter in the case of the timeless one? A devotee from Bombay who, in fact, got together a group of devotees of Bhagawan was on a visit to Tiruvannamalai. Visit, perhaps, is a wrong word. It is the sacred *sthala*, where the *achala* Ramana stayed routed. Unmoving, but not immobile, stationary but not static, radiant yet inconspicuous, the place is a condensed physical extension of the Mouna Swami, as Maharshi was often called. Just as he never left the place, once he reached there, he never ceased to pull to himself people from all walks of life from several nationalities and countries.

There was something magical in the attraction Maharshi had; there was something miraculous. The charisma drew seekers even without any prior knowledge or premonition of what silent subtle transformation Bhagawan would bring about. If he taught through silence, he also taught without their guessing that they were being taught. The quality of his teaching, like his unfathomable compassion, was never strained but fell gently. Unnoticed, unseen but felt in depths of one's being.

The Bombay devotee came for the *darshan* of Bhagawan, along with his wife and their child who was just nine months old. The word used is *darshan*, not seeing. *Darshan* is something beyond seeing. For that, of course, the eye is needed but is not indispensable. "They have eyes but see not; they have ears but hear not!" say the scriptures. The thing however is, is Bhagawan seeing you? That is the thing. In that seeing is the mystery. It explains the impact. Don't think it is a diversion. But I must record my experience. I was just fifteen. And one day I saw the photograph of Bhagawan on the front cover of a journal called *Swatantra* edited by the famed journalist the late Khasa Subba

Rao. What struck me most and remained etched in my consciousness, shall I say my inner being, were his eyes! They haunt you; they are clear, transparent, not staring at you, but caressing you. "You are my child! Give all your burdens to me, I shall joyfully carry them! You got onto my train! Keep the burden down, the train will carry it!" That is the assurance they give you. Those eyes.

At fifteen I could hardly guess all this; not that I do now, but I glimpse it – the unfathomable impact of *darshan*. If a photograph could tune your being with such vibrations – *spandana*, as followers of Kashmir Shaivisam call it, – what must have been the impact of seeing him in the physical frame? (But should we regret? I suppose no. For, a photograph means writing with light! And what could be a better subject for that process than Bhagawan!)

The Bombay devotee, his wife and child had *darshan*, and went for breakfast. Shall we say *Prasad* rather than breakfast? For, often it was Bhagawan himself who prepared the dishes! In a variety of ways which included " recycling." (This we shall talk about at the proper place). They finished eating and went to wash their hands. The child was left in the hall. They came back but the child could not be seen.

"What happened! Oh my God! Where is the child? Has anything untoward happened?" the devotee almost shouted in despair.

"What will happen? The child can't walk. He can only crawl," rejoined the wife. "Let us look around," she added. Perhaps she was not panicky. It is anybody's guess whether she had more faith in Bhagawan.

Filled with panic, rendered totally helpless, the devotee started shouting the name of the child, "Ramana! Ramana!" Until now, we are not told that the child's name was the same as that of Bhagawan's. That is the key to the incident. Moreover, look at the strange fact; will a nine-month-old child be capable of responding to his name? Does he recognize his name, even if he hears it? Contrast it with another. Even if you recognize the name, will you associate it with Bhagawan or the child? The child has no chance of knowing who Ramana is. Suppose we know and associate it with Bhagawan himself. Is it something beyond knowing the name? There is no need to speculate like this. The 'real' Ramana Bhagawan responded to his call (I mean the father's call), we are told 'immediately.' And the child was found near the well in the compound. The child was restored to the parents. The father was happy. But a nagging remained. (It remains for us also!) Why did Bhagawan respond? Did he really think that the father had called him and not the child? Can he dare to call Bhagawan by his name? It is unthinkable. Obviously, Bhagawan mistook his call.

What a trick the minds of even the most devoted play on them? On one side we have faith that Ramana is Bhagawan. Obviously, he is omniscient, knows everything. Or rather, chooses to know if there is need. Then, on the other, *maya* traps us. In moments of crisis, that knowledge is eclipsed, or, so we think.

But the ending of the incident reveals that the eclipse is necessary. Bhagawan was designing the incident to tell a profound

No Difference

truth. The narrator tells us, "Bhagawan was quick to read the devotee's mind and told him, 'why did you feel puzzled when I responded to the call? Is there any difference between this Ramana (meaning himself) and that Ramana (meaning the child)."

Can there be a simpler, more natural revelation of a profound truth than this? "Out of the mouths of babes and suckling," they say, "comes the truth."

But then can we, like that child, be innocent and yet experience the truth Bhagawan showed?

2

Witness The Passing Show: It`s *Cinemaya*

I always wonder whether Maharshi saw any movie. So far as I could guess, no he didn't. But, then, I am assuming that to see physically is the only way of seeing. This is true, so far as Sri Ramakrishna was concerned. He was fond of the theatre and he saw the religious plays that his, in many ways a unique disciple, Girish Chandra Ghosh wrote, directed and often acted in. And the Master declared when he was asked after seeing *Chaitanya Leela*, how he felt, " I saw no difference between the actor and Chaitanya whose role he enacted. All is one." He also went into ecstasy often 'seeing' the play.

Bhagawan did something else. Even when he, presumably didn't 'see,' he *saw through* the cinema for what it is. An analogue for self-enquiry.

It happened in this way. A question which often confronts us, how do we arrive at the 'real' self or 'I' in the midst of this vast world of activity, which is often confusing and rarely clear;

activity marked by paradoxes, by conflicting emotions, repressions, conflicts? We dream and it appears real so long as it lasts; we wake up and think it is a dream. But then a 'dream tiger,' as Sri Ramakrishna said, is no dream so far as its emotional impact is concerned. We wake up trembling with fear which is neither illusory nor a fantasy. It is 'real.'

Suppose there is something which is a mix of waking and dreaming? Or something which we willingly accept as 'real'. This, moreover, is not a drama in which we can see 'real' actors but a series of moving pictures on a screen? Motion pictures, we call them. The actors on the screen, at the time we see them, are in 'reality' not there on the screen. But if they are not there how do we get drugged to experience they are there? In fact, besides, we pay money to have this experience.

To part with money to experience nothing that is real. And if millions of people all over the world are, almost, 'mad' about this, there must be, the Maharshi knew, a function implicit in that. A function, moreover, which can be an extraordinarily effective tool for awakening to what 'I' is.

Let us put the whole thing thus: Bhagawan asks and we answer:

B: Do you watch movies ?
D: No, I don't. They are a waste of time and nothing is gained by seeing all those shadows on the screen.
B: I don't think you should have a negative attitude towards anything. Everything in nature that exists naturally or is designed by human intelligence is functional.

D: I don't think cinema can be of any use.
B: Why not? Just tell me what is the first thing that happens when the film has to begin?
D: Lights are off. There is darkness all around. In that darkness only we can see the screen light up.
B: Then, can't we say that it is out of darkness only that we see or pray for light? That this could be taken as movement from *Tamas* to *Jyothi*. Isn't it the way we pray?
D: Where is the Vedic prayer of an exalted nature and where is this frivolous show that is a film!
B: Frivolous? I find nothing that is frivolous in this universe. From everything we can draw lessons for self-enquiry.
D: Such a serious subject and drawing lessons or, shall I say clues, for "Who am I?"
B: Yes. Surely.
D: I accept. I have implicit faith in you.
B: It is not a question of faith. It is simply analysing carefully whatever you experience. Do not say that only certain experiences are valuable to know the answer to the question "Who am I?" Right.
D: Yes, Master.
B: No need to call me Master. We are all the same. OK? Now tell me who is seeing the film?
D: 'I' am seeing the film.
B: Are you sure your answer is complete. Just think.
D: 'I' am sure about *this* 'I' which is seeing the film.
B: Right. Are you seeing items which this 'I' of yours wants to see? Are you sure that your 'will' counts in what is being seen or, rather, being shown?

D: No. How can I see what I would like to see? I haven't made the film; *what I am shown I see.*

B: Then you are merely a witness, not the creator of the story, music, actions etc. Right?

D: I suppose so. I am sure about one thing. I don't have a choice when I decide to see a movie, a particular movie I want to see. I go in with some expectations, no doubt.

B: Are your expectations fulfilled?

D: Not always. Often the movie is bad. I feel I wasted my money and my time. But sometimes I feel happy. It is a good movie.

B: I am not bothered about a good movie. I am only concerned with a bad movie. How do you respond to something which you do not like? That is, it does not come up to what you expect to see?

D: I feel frustrated.

B: But does your frustration matter? Will you go to the director and tell him this is not the way to make it?

D: I don't. Why should he listen to me?

B: Even in the case of a good movie, do you go to the maker(s) and thank them?

D: Of course, I feel pleased and not necessarily to the extent that I try to go and thank him

B: Suppose, you do have an opportunity to go and do both complain or complement. Does it change anything?

D: My going doesn't make any difference. The director's response is a guess. He may feel unhappy if I say it is a bad movie. Or, even if I say it is a good movie; that's that.

B: In other words, what the director makes you experience is a fact. Your responses in either case are of no consequence. Suppose, you go to the movie without any expectations then you won't be disappointed. And not being disappointed, you do not feel any sense of frustration. Right?

D: Yes.

B: Since you are merely experiencing what the director has created, don't you think that it is better neither to expect nor to feel disappointed or fulfilled?

D: Yes, I think so. Now that you explain it 'I' think it better to remain neutral and accept whatever is shown. I mean experience whatever is shown.

B: Good. Don't you think that two simple facts from an experience which you called frivolous can be learnt?

D: Do please tell me.

B: Why should 'I' tell you? You should rely on your own experience.

D: Now that you put it that way, I think I can venture to say: whatever happens, happens. Whatever does not happen will not happen. So there is no need to feel worried about what happens.

B: That's right. That's a fact I told my mother when she came to take me back to our place.

D: That's what I remembered. But I didn't know you could confirm what I heard by experiencing a movie!

B: Everything illumines and radiates knowledge of the Self. Remember that. And what is the second thing?

D: If I am not expecting something which I like, then I feel no disappointment. Suppose, I simply see what is being given, I am a spectator. A witness.

B: That's right. You are a witness of something strange. That also is important. Most important.

D: You mean, Bhagawan ....

B: Yes, the white screen. Whatever event is projected it shows. It has no attachment to good movies or detachment from bad movies. Whatever has to be projected, it projects. But it remains neutral, unchanging. The show is over. The screen assumes its original color white, which is no color at all. And only an empty white screen can show other colors. If it has a color of its own, then where is the show? Shall we say that it is the Self that illumines everything without requiring any apparatus to illumine itself.

D: But our experiences of emotions are real. I feel miserable when the hero is in trouble and feel happy when he triumphs over the villain.

B: That's true. They are tendencies which are already there in you. So they are activated and you feel the *latent* emotions which we call *Samskaras*.

D: But the emotions, whatever their nature, are experienced always as pleasurable. Even in pain there is pleasure!

B: That's why you can call it not just cinema, but Cine*maya*. It is illusion but points to the reality. Remember the lamp that projects everything. That's a pointer to who am 'I'; I am the Self that witnesses without getting caught. It enjoys but does not get attached. Or, rather, it balances attachment and detachment.

D: Does it mean the realized Self also experiences these qualities?
B: Yes. But with awareness that it is all a show – a passing show, for the unchanging 'I'.

3

The Mason`s Prayer

Bhagawan is, for many, a *jnani* who followed the *jnana marga* of *vichara* – enquiry into "Who am I?" But he was a different type of *jnani*. Love and compassion flowed from his heart, engulfing everyone. Even those who were keen about knowing the subtleties of this path were simply overwhelmed by his love, by his care and concern for everyone.

The strange thing is, there was no need for any kind of even remote awareness of any spiritual quest. A throb of yearning, a pulse of intense desire for darshan is enough. The concerned person may not be even aware of what Bhagawan really meant for hundreds of people who came to him. That didn't matter to Bhagawan. "His desire is intense. He wants to see me. That is enough."

Sri Ramakrishna used to sing a song: "Ask for *mukti*. I shall give you instantly. Ask me for love. I have to think twice." So precious is the supreme love (*parama prema*) of a Master.

At the time of this incident, Bhagawan was recovering from an accident. He was coming down Arunachala one day. Don't underestimate a dog! It is invariably associated with Dattatreya. And the four dogs which followed or accompanied him always, represented, they say, the four Vedas. But this dog, true to its instinct, ran suddenly and pounced on a squirrel and tried to catch him. Bhagawan instantly reacted. He put a stick between them to prevent the squirrel being harmed. This made him lose his balance and he fell. A collarbone broke.

For nearly a month Bhagawan was bedridden. His love for the so-called animals begs description. The cow Lakshmi, monkeys, peacocks – how many were touched and blessed by his love! His highest transcendental state blended with an acute, all encompassing environmental awareness. Didn't the entire cosmos remain imbedded in this majestic being!

The collar had hardly healed when he decided to go up the hill Arunachala. Two devotees asked Bhagawan:

> "Give us permission to go to Skandasramam. We wish to have its darshan again and bathe our consciousness in that place sanctified by your radiant presence. Do we have your permission to pay the visit?"

One can imagine Bhagawan's joy. Before he came down the sacred hill Arunachala, Skandasramam was his abode. Sitting there in total but vibrant silence enjoying the breathtaking spectacle of the hill, Bhagawan felt totally in tune with the cosmos. "It isn't a hill. It is the *Virat swarupa* of my Father, Siva himself!" he used to say. We recall the thrill he felt all over his body and being when one of his relatives simply gave him the information, "I returned after visiting Arunachala!" The word 'Arunachala' rang like a celestial melody in his ears. It was the magic of the *Anahata*, the unstruck but felt cosmic sound. The relative's information led to transformation, indeed.

That is Skandasramam. When I visited it, I could, if not fully, experience something of the radiance surrounding the place. Hallowed by the presence of Bhagawan, it brought me epiphanic moments of what it could have been with Bhagawan's physical presence. It was on the hill that the great sage Kavyakantha Ganapathi Muni discovered this radiant being. And it was Ganapathi Muni who declared him Bhagawan Ramana. Venkataraman became Ramana Bhagawan.

So much lay behind the epic narrative of the hill and Skandasramam.

> "Yes. Why not? Do go.
> It's a pilgrimage. It's not just going up the hill," said Bhagawan.

But he asked Rangaswamy, his attendant:

> "Shall we also go, it has been quite some time since I went up!"
> "How can we go up in your present condition? The wound is yet to heal and doctors don't want you to have any strain!" a shocked Rangaswamy replied.

The devotees agreed. And with Bhagawan's permission they started on the journey. Perhaps they were not worried because Rangaswamy was as obedient as stern in the present context. He will not allow Bhagawan to take a risk.

But who knows Bhagawan's *sankalpa*? Who can guess what makes him do certain things in a certain way? His is the *leela* and behind every act there is a motive, a function.

The two devotees climbing the hill casually looked back. They were shocked and petrified. Bhagawan was coming up, following them with his attendant. The devotees just couldn't stomach this. One ran down panting and asked Bhagawan:

> "Why are you coming up in this hot sun? And you are not well! Oh my God! We should, ourselves, have stopped coming up. Then this wouldn't have happened!"

By this time Bhagawan was seen sitting under the shade of a tree. It was quite hot and Bhagawan appeared tired. The devotees pleaded with him to go back. He refused, intently looking at a worker doing some masonry job. The mason's glance fell upon Bhagawan sitting at a distance. His face lighted up with a joy that is spontaneous, natural. Perhaps, he couldn't believe his eyes. He fell to the ground and prostrated to Bhagawan. Dumb for a minute, he broke into speech:

> "Oh my Bhagawan! What a rare, blessed fortune to have your *darshan*! You climbed up the hill in this condition to see this lowly creature! Do I deserve this compassion!"

Yes. The devotees felt the same. Even the celestial beings, the many sages and saints living on the hill in either visible or invisible forms, must have felt blessed. Meantime, the mason ran down some distance brought some water and eatables for Bhagawan and the devotees.

One can imagine Bhagawan's smile, soft and serene and yet illumining the entire being with a strange light. The eyes sparkled with joy and he said:

> "Yes, yes. It is your prayer which brought me here. Indeed, it pulled me here. I cannot resist a genuine desire to see me. Its compulsion is irresistible."

The devotees were totally lost. What was that earnest prayer which brought Bhagawan up the hill? In this heat and with a wound still to heal completely, what made him bear this discomfort, this obvious strain? Curiosity overpowered the devotees and they asked:

> "What was his prayer, Bhagawan? Was his longing so intense to see you that you came all the way? Couldn't he have come down the hill, without making you come up?"
> "Intense longing, yes. But there was another reason, too," said Bhagavan.

The devotees perked up their ears.

> "You know we had that function regarding the rising of pillars for the New Hall?" he asked.
> "Yes, we do. We had a special worship, too," they said.
> The doctor gave me permission and I came to the function. It was quite a gathering. Among them was this mason also. And do you know what he thought seeing that function?" asked Bhagawan

Of course, they didn't know. But Bhagawan knew. Inside out of everyone that came to him, he knew the innermost inarticulate and insistent longings of everyone. And he fulfilled them. Bhagawan resumed:

"The mason thought, 'Bhagawan himself came to this function and blessed it. Will Bhagawan come and see with what patience and devotion I am doing the same work at Skandasramam? This is a dream. I am a simple mason and how can Bhagawan come? But I can't help praying that he should bless me by coming to see my work for Skandasramam. It would indeed be a miracle!"

Bhagawan paused:

"Can I resist such an earnest wish? Who am I? Am I a great person? or a celebrity? I simply wear a loincloth and sit doing nothing! But his desire moved me intensely. And I came, even though it caused me great discomfort. But pain is nothing in the face of love. Don't you think?"

The devotees were left wondering looking at this lion in a loincloth, sitting there with a wound on his collarbone, but beaming that he could fulfill the desire of the mason.

But today, after so many years, every one of us knows that this is the truth and nothing but the truth. Bhagawan comes, provided you allow him to come. The option is ours. Or, rather, even if we close our heart's doors, he will enter like the butter thief, Sri Krishna, silently and stealthily! If he puts a stick to prevent a squirrel from getting hurt, will he not do the needful for us when we really surrender?

4

"The Body Is Mortal: Why Feel Sad? I Am With You!"

Whenever you (I mean myself) plunge into the vast ocean of the recollections of Ramana by devotees, you can't help one thing. You shed tears of joy! What sweetness it tastes! Rarely you find such an experience. For me, only one other book unfailingly gives that experience: *Kathamrita, The Gospel of Sri Ramakrishna*.

As I said, if you have tears to shed, there is no more fitting context which warrants them! To see Ramana Bhagawan's face is enough to be stirred to the depths of your being; every incident that you read brings about vibrations in the consciousness that are difficult to describe and impossible to evoke.

The way to absorb such a one as Bhagawan, is to shun thought and fill the entire being with every detail. But it is only in a vibrant void, *sunyata*, that Bhagawan's silence is articulate! And the test of absorption is to apply what you read in comparable contexts. Such a way only is capable of making Bhagawan a perennial presence.

This I could sense in one incident connected with the very experience which "brought enlightenment to Bhagawan, the so-called death incident."

The devotee concerned, Akhilandamma, heard about the Brahmana Swami, the name by which Bhagawan was known then; and he was just twentyfour years old and lived in the Virupaksha caves. The moment she heard about the young Swami, some intuition told her she must go and see him.

How did Bhagawan appear to her? "What a sight he was! For the first time I saw the magnetic Lord who draws the minds of those who see him!" Above all, though unwashed, unkempt and covered with dust, "his body glowed like gold!"

I don't know whether a photograph of those days exists and even if it exists does the "inner eye" require a physical prop to "see" what Akhilandamma saw and put it in words? "Burnished gold." Glowed like gold! The description bears out the need for the "inner eye".

A strange event confirms this. It was a full moon day. Very auspicious for seekers of peace and love. The widow was taking some *bhiksha* for Bhagawan and going up Arunachala when she encountered a Swami. He knew her spiritual potential, obviously, and told her:

> "Today it is very auspicious, very congenial for a person like you travelling on the path of the spirit. I am sure you are taking *bhiksha* for the Brahmana Swami. Right?"

"Yes. Swami," replied the lady.

"Then why don't you do one thing?"

"What should I do? Seeing the Brahmana Swami and serving some food to him is enough for me. Isn't it the greatest good fortune to have *darshan* and feed him?" "True. But you just ask him to give you *upadesa*. It is your great fortune to see such a supreme being on a full moon day!"

"*Upadesa*? I don't know what it is."
"The Mouna Swami knows, you just request him for *Diksha*. That is enough. And listen to what he says," said the Swami and left.

The devout lady took the food for Bhagawan as usual and later bowed to him and taking courage into her hands, she said, "Bhagawan tell me something." Perhaps, Bhagawan was surprised. He stared at her and asked, "What do you want me to tell you?"

The apparent question didn't matter. The very voice and words emanating from Bhagawan thrilled her. An inexpressible joy coursed through her veins. Can any question to another question create such impact? Yes, it could. For, she could never expect an answer. She put the question without knowing what it meant. Therefore, the question of Bhagawan answering the question was, for her, immaterial. There was no *sabda vichara* or *kuthuhala* curiosity in her. She simply had that precious thing: faith and the eagerness to serve Bhagawan.

Then, Bhagawan knew what the question was and was aware of what she needed. He simply said, "be, without leaving yourself." What was the impact? Something, nothing short of a miracle. Akhilandamma did not understand the meaning or the significance. But it was *upadesa* nevertheless. The words Bhagawan uttered entered the consciousness like tides, she said. They went on shining with a radiance, almost incantatory, like a mantra.

What is the secret of the magic? We can, perhaps, say it is of the meaning one called *paravak*. It is beyond words, beyond denotation of meaning. The meaning the words carry need not be known before its impact is felt! Do we know what components have gone into the medicines we use (alas! there are special chocolates for many these days) to register its impact on our body? Do we know how to fly an airplane before we enjoy its flight into space? Perhaps, the magic is for devotees like Akhilandamma Intuition courses through every vein, every pore of their bodies. No wonder, the staunch devotee told her later, "though I didn't understand what Bhagawan had said, I *immediately experienced* the state the words were indicating without ever really understanding what they meant! I came to understand through this experience that in Bhagawan's benign presence a single gracious utterance can produce the fruit and fulfillment of all spiritual practices such as *sravana* (hearing), *manana* (thinking or reflection), *nidhidyasana* (contemplation of abidance).

As if this is not enough, Bhagawan's grace came in the form of a fitting finale. The blessed lady heard that Bhagawan was not well and almost "the last" days had arrived. She rushed to see him, but her mind was burdened with unbearable grief. Will the beacon light of her entire life be extinguished forever? How could she bear the prospect of not seeing him?

Perhaps, her mind raced through the experiences either manifest or latent, she went through. And imagine her enormous good fortune of serving food to Bhagawan for *forty years*! She fed his *annamaya kosha* and in return Bhagawan activated her *vijnanamaya kosha*, the sheath, the pure experience of which makes us, they say, beyond knowledge and ignorance.

When Akhilandamma saw the body lying there without any movement, it was a sight that cut at the root of all her pent up emotion. She cried, "Bhagawan! Oh Bhagawan. You have decided to quit the body! But who will look after this poor widow! One who knows nothing about anything which you taught, they say. What should I do, Bhagawan!" And unable to control herself, she left the room.

But that was not the end. A devotee came within a few minutes.

"Akhilandamma! Just wait. Bhagawan has a message for you!"

The woman stopped in her tracks and stared at him. For a minute, perhaps even in her wildest imagination, she could hardly think that in that state too, Bhagawan would remember her. But how could she even imagine that he who gave her illumination without initiation, would forsake her. As Sri Ramakrishna puts it: Ordinary saints are like ordinary snakes: they catch a frog but they cannot be swallowed totally. They are stuck in the throat. But avatharas, mahanubhavas are like king cobras: Once they catch they swallow the frog, lock, stock and barrel.

> "Don't you want to hear the message? Stop staring and listen. Bhagawan wanted me to tell you …."
> "Please tell me," she said, her throat choking with tears.
> "Why do you feel sorry, for this mortal body?" that is what he wanted me to tell you.

Akhilandamma's response none can put into words. But she tried:

"It occurred to me that Bhagawan was consoling me, saying, 'don't worry about the body, I am always your saviour!'"

"I am always your saviour! Listen to my words in the interior." Don't you feel that they are not meant for Akhilandamma alone? "Am I not there with you all? I pervade the entire cosmos. I sat as *achala* unmoving, in *Arunachala* but I am, in fact, everywhere. Nothing can contain or confine me. I just don't knock on the door. I enter even if you inadvertently close it. *I am.*"

Let it be so. Amen to that. *Can* we say more? *Need* we say more?

5

Where Is Our Own Pencil?

"Where is *our own* pencil? See where it is and bring it," said Bhagawan.

We are somewhat surprised initially by this. Why "our own"? Can one imagine this great Mahatma who had no sense of 'I' use an expression indicating ownership? But carefully note the word "our". He didn't use "my".

But, first of all, let us see why he wanted this "our pencil" to be found. A devotee brought some expensive pencils for Bhagawan.

"Bhagawan! These are good pencils. Please use them." He said and left, taking his blessings.

Devotees never come with empty hands to Mahatmas. They give something or the other, they call it "pranami." Bhagawan took them, found them to be really nice and said:

"These are good pencils. Keep them carefully. But we have our own pencil. Please find it and bring it to me."

Somebody took the pencils, placed them in a box and searched for the one Bhagawan asked for. He found one in a wooden box and gave it to Bhagawan.

You may ask why this fuss? There is a point which immediately we may not grasp. Did the person who searched for the pencil make sure that the pencil that Bhagawan asked for is the same that he found before giving it to Bhagawan? In other words, he equated whatever he found with "Bhagawan's pencil". He didn't even ask, "is this the *one* you asked for, Bhagawan?" He simply assumed, or it seems to me, and this is the assumption he *automatically* made. Doesn't it show a little bit of, I don't know whether one can call it so, carelessness?

Bhagawan was one of those who never made any distinction between worldly wisdom and the so-called spirituality. He was meticulous about everything. His words were precise, unambiguous in any matter. Whether pencil or pranayama, it never made any difference to him. Everything had to be exact. Moreover, there is another point which is of great value in everything, listening. "Our", must not have registered in the mind of the devotees. "Sravana" was casual.

Bhagawan looked at the pencil for a minute and said:

> "Why this one? Devaraja Mudaliar gave this? I asked for our own pencil. It must be somewhere there. Give that to me. But first put this also safely somewhere."

Very categorical reply. "Safely". Very important word. I know what it means. Personally, I misplace things in my haste to find something I need at that moment and in that context. Most of us, I console myself, are like this.

Everywhere they searched but couldn't find it. "Search properly and find it," said Bhagawan. Don't we feel delighted and at the same time somewhat dazed by the language. "Search properly" you can apply straightaway to "Who am I?", Bhagawan's mantra for self-realization. And if you search properly you are bound to find 'It'. So, the proper search is common register. But the same process of finding a pencil marks the quest for the Self, the abiding Self. Once we are centered there, every act acquires sanctity and thoroughness. The energy is, perhaps, the same.

Normally we do not bother about small things and yet quote, dutifully, the Gita definition of "Yoga is skill in action." Any action should be done skillfully, with care and concern. When Bhagawan said, "search properly and find it," this is an example of the dictum. One is reminded of Sri Ramakrishna's advice: When the umbrella he used was not kept in its proper place, he took the person to task. He added, "even in darkness you should be able to locate it when you stretch your hand for it!"

This was not the only thing. When Devaraja Mudaliar, a staunch and close devotee saw this, he thought that Bhagawan was making a fuss. He asked, "I don't think you should worry about your pencil. Aren't all these pencils your own?" Very pertinent question. Yes, anything that was given to Bhagawan belonged to him. Or, we think so, but we are wrong.

Bhagawan's logic is entirely different. He explained:

> "If it is our own pencil, we are not bothered where it is kept. But the pencil I use, someone gave it and it was

found somewhere. No one claimed it. So we can say it is our own. We are not answerable to anyone. So we can use it."

One can easily imagine Mudaliar's predicament. Perhaps, he didn't know what a strict ethical issue was involved — so far as Maharshi was concerned. In short, Maharshi made a distinction between owning on one's own and using someone else's gift.

Are we splitting hair about this incident? That, it appears so, is the ethical crudity we are used to — thanks to consumerism. Bhagawan also makes another aspect clear:

"We are not important people. We need not, moreover, pass any examination. Why do we need such pencils? That pencil is more than enough for our writing work."

And finally, "Bhagawan's pencil" was found. But note the word "need" which is emphasized. In the Yoga practices there is a particular injunction called "aparigraha", non-acceptance of gifts. That is, I feel, what is shown by Bhagawan. It's just not mere "simplicity" that Suri Nagamma, who recorded the incident, calls it. That it is. More than that, it shows the amazing ability to do with the irreducible minimum and yet constantly sport in the vast ocean of Chidananda—the bliss, the beatitude that comes inevitably which in the case of Bhagawan, attracted a vast number of seekers magnetically.

Incidentally, don't underestimate the pencil itself as a pointer to skills, either soft or spiritual. Paulo Coelho, the famous author of the novel *The Alchemist*, tells the story of a grandmother who shows to her grandson what we can learn from a pencil. The grandmother says, that more than the writing she was doing with the pencil, the pencil itself has important lessons to teach. For instance, we sharpen it which makes "the pencil suffer a little." But the end product of this suffering is greater sharpness. "Learn to bear pain and sorrow," like the pencil, she says, "to become a better person."

Moreover, writing with a pencil makes erasing mistakes easier. Doesn't it suggest correcting mistakes as a necessary part of "the road to justice," and to liberation. Similarly, in a pencil what is vital is the interior lead. "So pay attention to what is happening inside you." Bhagawan's injunction indeed.

"Above all," says Coelho, "If you look at things in this way" at everything and every experience, "a person is always at peace with the world."

"At peace with the world!" Can there be a more radiant example of this than Bhagawan?

Don't we thank the pencil and learn like the proverbial Avadhuta, from everything – trivial or tremendous, pleasant or unpleasant ... whatever it is.

6

Everything Is Alive, Pulsing With Life

Once I heard something amazing. A photograph was lying on the table and a person started drumming on it. Another who observed this was horrified.

> "Don't do it please," the other person almost shouted. "It will hurt the person. Our mentor."
> "Our mentor?" the other asked, incredulously.
> "Yes. He remains anonymous. Not many know him or he does not wish to be known. But he is very ordinarily extraordinary. Let it go. But once I heard him saying that when someone was doing just what you are doing now, he felt it on his body. He was, at that moment, somewhere, far away."
> "You believe that?"
> "I do, without any trace of doubt."
> "You mean to say that a photograph is no different from the subject in the photo?"
> "Yes. So far as he is concerned."

Everything Is Alive, Pulsing With Life

I know this is the truth. But often I wondered whether we could find any parallel to it. Of course, I am familiar with a similar incident but much more moving in the life of Sri Ramakrishna. When two boatmen came to blows over a fierce quarrel and one fellow hit the other severely on the back, Sri Ramakrishna sitting in his room in Dakshineswar temple garden, sprang to his feet and cried with unbearable pain, as though stung by a scorpion. When the disciples asked the Great Master, he showed his back where there were clear traces of the boatmen's hitting. He then explained to them that the entire cosmos is interconnected and shows on his own body!

One morning Bhagawan was on his way back from the cowshed, the abode of his favorite cows, when he saw an inmate, K, cutting down the ripe coconuts from the trees in the compound of the Ashram. Merrily, K was going about his job when Bhagawan passed by.

A context very familiar wherever there are coconut trees. It is done regularly not just there but everywhere. I was myself witness to this many times when coconuts were being pulled down from the trees. It was the Godavari delta and the coconuts were quite large and full of water and pulp. Heavenly to taste! It must have been tastier in Bhagawan's ashram! (Sorry, Bhagawan never claimed anything as his own! But when language is used, we can only speak that way!).

The observant eye of Bhagawan noticed everything. This context was no exception. He asked the "coconut puller":

"What are you using to pluck the coconuts? Is it a rod? Does it have a bamboo bit or an iron point at its end?"

Does it matter what point it has? Whether iron or bamboo, the end is to pluck the coconuts. So why the question? But one should always remember one thing, Bhagawan, known for his silence as communication never breaks it unless something is needed to be drawn attention to. Usually, something profound, even when the context appears to be commonplace.

"It's an iron sickle I'm using, Swami. It cuts at the root and it is easy to pull off the coconuts," replied K.

What other answer can we expect? This is very common. In Telugu, it is called "Kodavali," iron sickle. It is very sharp, so sharp as to be almost murderous in its impact. No wonder, Bhagawan asked something amazingly profound:

"Don't you think, the trees will be severely hurt by the sharp iron sickle? If you put a bamboo bit at the end of the rod, you can pull out the coconuts equally well, but without hurting them."

The man doing the job must have gaped at Bhagawan in dismay! Trees getting hurt? Iron point hurts more? Whoever heard of such a thing? The iron sickle has been in use for a long time. What is strange about it?

Obviously, the 'cutter' didn't get the point of what Bhagawan said. He never enquired why he made such a remark. He understood the meaning of the words but their significance never registered. The same applies to us; words and their meanings are clear. *Sabda Vichara* is, relatively manageable, but then does it lead to *Atmavichara*? Inquiry into the Self?

Moreover, the man went on with the job. No change in the instrument. The analogy suggests itself; do we, interested in self-inquiry, follow Bhagawan's words? We appreciate them, admire them, but I'm not sure we take them seriously. There is intellectual appreciation, but nothing of its results gets into life. Though it sounds negative, the truth is that alone; words do not seem to become live centers of transforming consciousness. What could be the nature of the person who continued to do what Bhagawan gently suggested should not be done? And why this indifference? Is it due to ignorance of the way or the manner in which Bhagawan advises – gently, without any offence meant? (There are exceptions, of course !). Or is it due to over-confidence in one's own judgment (which perhaps we can say borders on arrogance!)?

See also the irony; seekers from far off places of many nationalities and faiths, taking immense trouble, come to Bhagawan to listen to what he says, and follow, in their own way, to the extent they are capable of, what he advises in matters of self-realization. And a person living in the very place disregards what he says and goes on doing the same thing, cutting coconuts with an iron sickle.

But as my mentor, Sri Ram, would say – what man cannot do or for some reason is reluctant to do, Nature itself does in her own way. Like the recent Tsunami!

A week passed. K was still at the job and the iron sickle was employed merrily by K. But lo and behold! One coconut 'detached' itself and fell on the forehead of the man. The nose was injured severely. The pain was unbearable. Was it Nature's way of tilting the scales?

Perhaps, yes. But why a week's delay? Why could the justice not be speedy? An analogy suggests itself: did Sri Krishna punish Sisupala immediately? He gave a concession of hundred mistakes. And for Kamsa, too, the right and ripe moment has to come for things to right themselves.

But, I always wondered why Bhagawan did not prevent the man from continuing to do the thing and not replace the instrument to cut coconuts. Why did he remain detached, neutral? Several answers are possible. The one which seems to me most important is, one has to learn the hard way. Experience of hard lessons necessary for living do not come from goody-goody soft skills. If words are not enough then deeds are imperative.

The same is the case with enquiry into "Who am I?" One has to go the whole hog oneself. One has to tread the path oneself. There are no substitutes, no deputized people doing it for you. So, in this case, in everything in Nature, self-enquiry and experience are integrally linked.

When the coconut incident, injuring the cutter, was reported to Bhagawan, his immediate response was expressing pity and compassion for the injured man. But, then, in his characteristic way, he put the whole incident into perspective by his remarks: "The man will now know what it means to be hurt. Now, at least, I hope he will realize how much pain his iron sickle must have inflicted on the trees."

"They don't complain," he added.

Yes. Tree don't complains but give us ungrudgingly whatever they can, shade, fruit etc. They are hurt but they help us to heal by the products they generate.

Above all, they are all pulsing with life, the same life which flows through our veins pervades everything in Nature. It doesn't mean that we can get things like coconuts without some pain, but can't we minimize the pain? The local anesthetic is grace and compassion.

Jagdish Chandra Bose experimented and proved, in Aldous Huxley's memorable words, that "the inanimate is alive". But Bhagawan went a step further. He showed how the so-called inanimate can punish if needed.

7

Be God Yourself!

The man was extremely angry with Bhagawan. Indeed, he was shaking with rage. Why did he make him come all the way only to see that he was the same sadhu who visited him in Punjab? He must be deceiving many innocent people like himself, the man from Punjab felt .... Isn't it enough to see him at his own doorstep in Punjab but to take him for a ride like this! It was the limit.

The entire scenario is something which baffles us. It stretches the limits of faith and yet it is absolutely true. It has happened exactly as it was narrated.

It began with a devotee of Lord Krishna in Punjab. He was so devout, so firm in his faith, that even in the state of *sushupti* (deep sleep) he had visions of his beloved Lord, the Butter Thief of Brindavan. Krishna stole the devotee's heart and everything else, lock, stock and barrel. Perhaps, the man chose the right path, that of devotion. "*Kaliyuge Bhaktiyog*" – Sri Ramakrishna was fond of saying, for Kaliiyuga Bhakti is the proper path. That is because we are "*annagatha prana*" people. We subsist on food, not capable of severe austerities as seekers of earlier ages.

The devotee was working in the army and kept it balanced with his sadhana. Don't you think it is somewhat a strange combination, army and bhakti? Not that army people are not spiritual. It need not surprise us. For, the devotee's beloved Lord Sri Krishna taught the greatest philosophical scripture in world religions, *Bhagavad Gita,* when two armies were ranged against each other in Kurukshetra, and it was to the mighty, incomparable warrior Arjuna that the *Gita* was spoken!

However, he resigned from the army and devoted himself wholly to sadhana. He was intensely engaged in the quest to 'see' God. He visited many holy people and used to ask:

"Have you seen God? Can you show me God?"

Have you? Note the 'you'. It is not equivalent to asking, "Can God be seen?" He wanted the one who had seen God and not one who was merely talking about what is seeing. Sometimes, this talking is so impressive that we are deluded into equating talking beautifully as seeing directly. *Pratyaksha darshana*, that is what the Lord Krishna's devotee craved for. *Aparokshanubhuti* is also the word used.

The second question is much more important. Yes, some have seen God, but they may not be able to show us God. It is like they swam across the ocean and reached the other shore, but can they also take us across? Not just give us tips about swimming, but take us across, holding our hand, so to say. In short, perception about God is something, but *darshan* of God is something else.

Sri Ramakrishna used to say that realised people are of three kinds. He gave the example of a huge wall. Three persons reached the wall and wanted to climb and see what was on the other side of the wall. The first one climbed the wall and saw that a huge *mela* was going on. People were jumping with joy, enjoying everything there. The moment he saw the mart of joy, the carnival, he couldn't contain himself and jumped on to the other side shouting with great gusto.

The two standing on the ground were totally at a loss. What had he seen on the other side? Was there something irresistibly magical that he forgot his friends totally? But isn't it unfair, they thought – the two below.

The second friend climbed the wall. It was a bit difficult. But he did it. And saw what the first one saw. He too, was overjoyed. It was full of fun and frolic. There was no trace of sorrow anywhere in that garden of undefiled joy. But he remembered his friend below. He should also know and experience what was there that made the first one jump to the other side without bothering about the two friends below. Moreover, the third one waiting below, was full of *sraddha*, but not given to much energy. He needed help.

The second devotee came down, gave him a helping hand and asked him to do what was needed. This category of a real helper is scarce, and the army devotee was looking for such a one.

Then the miracle happened. A sadhu came for *bhiksha*. Sadhus rarely come to bless householders. The real sadhus, I mean. Sankaracharya says: the great Mahatmas move about the world for the welfare of the world like the spring season – *Vasantha ritu*.

The devotees gave him food and seizing the opportunity, the desperately seeking devotee asked the sadhu:

"Maharaj! Can I ask you for a favour?"
"Sure. You can. Tell me."
"Can you direct me to a sadhu or a Mahatma who is capable of showing God to me? I have met many, but they talk about everything else but not the thing I ask for!"

Instant came the reply:

"Yes. Bhagawan Ramana of Arunachala."

The name was enough. The seeker's whole body felt waves of joy flow through his veins. There was a strange thrill. "Ramana!" What a lovely name, he felt.

How do we explain this nearly incredible impact? Can anyone find the reason? Not just this particular case. Countless seekers just hear the name 'Ramana' and a strange electricity begins to flow. This is a phenomenon attested to by many, And to try to explain it is futile. We can only take consolation from Shakespeare's words: "There are more things in heaven and earth than are dreamt of in your philosophy!"

The sadhu left. And the devotee also left his village, finding out all the details about Arunachala and Tiruvannamalai. But his concern was how to get the money for such a long journey? From Punjab to Tamilnadu! Quite an expensive journey.

But when Nature finds that the need is genuine and sincere, it is unfailing in its help and guidance. I myself experienced this, not once but, many times. And I swear this is true to the hilt.

(Perhaps, if it is not a distraction, I would like to mention one such incident. Recently, I had to speak at the 4th International Conference on *Gita* held at Vijayawada. This was to be under the auspices and the blessings of one of the most respected sages: Ganapati Sachidananda Swamiji. Until then I had never had the darshan of this holy personage. I had read about him in his biography put together by Sri Kuppa, but that was quite some time back. I was desperate to get something recent. I didn't, of course, resort to prayer or any such thing. In spite of my desperation, I remembered what my mentor often told me: "If it is really needed, that thing will surely reach you. Nature never fails to do what is needed; not what is merely, in your view, desirable."

And so it happened. I visited a local bookstore. And staring at me – as soon as I stepped in – was a book on the experiences of western devotees of Swamiji! Elegantly produced, with a smiling, radiant figure of Swamiji on the cover, it was a treat to the eye and treasure trove for those devoted to such matters.)

The Punjab devotee got a needed break. A canteen in Madras wanted a caretaker and that too an ex-army man! He fitted the bill, got the job and landed in Titruvannamalai after a few days.

That is where he got angry. Why anger? The sadhu who visited their home and whom they fed devotedly was none other than Bhagawan himself! What a climax or, rather, anti-climax. He had come with high expectations and they were all dashed to the ground. Frustrated, he packed his bag and started out pronto.

But, does Bhagawan allow a sincere seeker to leave like that, abruptly, disappointed, frustrated. He may test severely but always examines the script liberally. Testing and trusting go together. And it happened; Bhagawan's concern started unrolling itself.

The devotee ran into an inmate of the ashram who was watching all this. He stopped him and said:

"My dear friend! Why are you leaving in a huff? Are you angry with Bhagawan? If so, it is for nothing."
"Explain yourself. I don't have much time to waste," the seeker of God said, with visible annoyance.
"Have some patience and listen to what I am saying. Bhagawan never left this place ever since he came here in 1896. Everyone knows it. You can check. He is *achala*, unmoving like his deity Arunchala Shiva."

There was gradually a change on the angry devotee's face. Maharshi never left Tiruvannamalai? Then how could he see him in far away Punjab, in his own house?

"In some mysterious way," the inmate continued, "Bhagawan came to bless you at your own place in Punjab. How fortunate, how blessed you are?"

The devotee gaped at him, speechless for some time. Then he rushed to Bhagawan. His heart bursting, again, with the intense longing to see God.

One can imagine Bhagawan's smile on seeing him again. He was familiar with devotees, seekers of all shapes and sizes, with varied temperaments. He could at a glance see through the potentialities. Now this devotee put again the same question to Bhagawan:

"Have you seen God? Can you show me God? Bhagawan!"

Bhagawan kept silent. There was something more the Punjab seeker had to say:

"Bhagawan! I am willing to pay any price. Your part of our agreement is to, enable me to see God!"

Bhagawan continued his silence. We know that his silence is more articulate than his speech. Indeed, as my mentor 'Sri Ram' once put it memorably: "Only when silence commits suicide, speech is born!" Silence is the most powerful weapon that, in the right context, is the most effective *spandana*! But here there was need to speak. The reason is simple, the devotee who came had intensity but was naïve. So he had to be given the right dosage, "the ultimate medicine".

Bhagawan broke his silence. His voice was firm and the words precise, decisive, pointed:

"You want to see God. Right?" he asked.
"Yes, Bhagawan. That is what brought me here. You know it."
"Yes. I do."
"I can enable you to not only see him but to be God."

One can imagine the shocking effect these ringing words must have had when they fell on the ears of the seeker. He was, to say the least, definitely puzzled.

"I want to see God. And you are saying you will enable me to be God myself! Strange!"

These, perhaps, were the thoughts that raced through his mind.

Bhagawan resumed:

"What is the use of a God who comes and goes? If he is a real God, he must be with you always."

God's abiding presence – that's what is to be sought, not intermittent glimpses or sporadic intimations. The presence should be abiding, and *achala* rock-like in its abidance. Seeing God is good, but far, far superior is his perennial presence felt in every pore of his body, in every crevice of awareness. Awareness that is abiding!

So many words for what Bhagawan said so directly and in such few words! But that is our predicament. This apart, what was the *spandana* in this seeker? "The words sank into his heart and he experienced the most wonderful feeling of bliss that he had ever known," it is said. They call it *Chidananda*, in Sanskrit.

What is God except *Ananda,* the bliss that defies description, the peace that passeth understanding? Experienced, without exception, in one's Self?

How come Bhagawan blessed him so soon and so spontaneously going all the way to Punjab while remaining at the same time in Arunachala? One unquestionable qualification is, disregard and indifference to miracles. Remember, in the beginning when he realized that Bhagawan and the guest who came were the same, he got angry. He never asked how was it possible to be at two places at the same time? In short, he wanted the real miracle – the Supreme Being abiding in his own Self. Nothing less, nothing more. He never compromised.

8

Turn Your Life Over To That

"Pin-drop silence pervades throughout the long hall. The sage remains perfectly still, motionless, quite undisturbed at our arrival .... I look full into the eyes of the seated figure, in the hope of catching his notice. They are dark-brown, medium-sized and wide open."

This is Paul Brunton's first impression of the Maharshi. Silence that matches the "still motionless figure." Or, rather, silence that radiates from this "figure itself." Later, he tells us, "His body is supernaturally quiet, as steady as a statue."

What is this stillness, quietude and what do we mean "supernaturally quiet?" Is there anything supernatural about Bhagawan? If not, how did Paul Brunton get this impression? Perhaps, he was searching for something which matches the presence of the many sadhus he saw already. He had already reflexes about what an Indian sadhu looks like, behaves, receives visitors, etc. And, of course, the siddhis, occult powers, they 'show' to impress, specially, a foreign visitor.

This sage does not fit into Brunton's search for secret India. This is Bhagawan's uniqueness. Indeed, another pet theory of Brunton receives a rude reversal. "It is an ancient theory of mine that one can take the inventory of a man's soul. But before those of the Maharishee, I hesitate, puzzled, baffled," he notes.

Baffled? Yes. Samsakaras are hard crusts. They rarely change. But then the Maharshi has his own way. When Brunton sees the stillness, the motionless figure he gets what, he frankly says almost every European does when face to face with something that does not fit into their categories. Hence, Brunton's blunt remark: "Is this man merely posing for the benefit of his devotees?"

Look at the net in which Brunton is caught; he has seen sadhus but never shed his spots of scepticism, of inevitable doubts arising from a congenital, almost ethnic, scepticism. If he thought of the stillness as a performative act, the thought that, perhaps, Maharshi's "mystical contemplation" was nothing more than meaningless vacancy.

Let us pause here. When I spoke about this to a friend of mine, he was perplexed. About what? About Brunton's misgivings and misperceptions.

> "*A Search in Secret India* is still popular. It is liked by many Indian readers and they think, still, that this is the book which introduced Maharshi to many seekers."
> "I am sure it does. That I am not denying," I said.
> "Then ……"
> "I am saying or trying to suggest that Bhagawan evoked varied responses and they are rooted in the theological beliefs into which one is born."

"And so ...."

"Initially such responses are active but they are neither rejected nor affirmed; they are simply neutralised."

"Neutralised?"

"Yes. Neutralised, if not totally dissolved. The reason is simple ...."

'What is that?"

"The reason; Bhagawan's core teaching is focussed on something which is inescapable, the sense of "I". None can do away with 'I'—whatever religion he or she belongs to, whatever attitude he or she holds towards his/her religion. And do you know ...."

"What more?"

"Even the scientist's so-called objectivity is also, we are now almost certain, an offshoot of his or her own subjectivity. In short, 'I'."

Brunton was both bewildered and fascinated because it is this strong bastion of "I" that started crumbling. (But it always comes back! That is the funny thing about 'I').

"My initial bewilderment, my perplexity at being totally ignored, slowly faded away," says Brunton, "as this strange fascination began to grip me firmly."

It now hardly matters whether he puts the questions which he came with.

"I know only that a steady river of quietness seems to be flowing near me, that a great peace is penetrating the inner reaches of my being and that my thought-tortured brain is beginning to arrive at some rest."

This is genuine. But is it free from the sub-conscious prediction for 'secrets,' mysteries and miracles? Perhaps not. His own account is ambivalent:

> "... I have personal reactions to other people. This dawning suspicion that the mysterious peace which has arisen within me must be attributed to the geographical situation in which I am placed is my reaction to the personality of the Maharishee. *I begin to wonder* whether, by some radio activity of the soul, some unknown telepathic process, the stillness which invades the troubled waters of my own soul really comes from him. Yet, he remains completely impassive, completely unaware of my very existence, it seems."

"Geographical situation, radio activity of the soul, unknown telepathic process..."

The real reason, it seems to me, is Brunton's powerful sense of identity was threatened. Without 'I' how can one exist? When Bhagawan asks him:

"You say I, 'I want to know.' Tell me who is that I?"

Promptly Brunton says, "I am afraid I do not understand your question."

Bhagawan advises, "Is it not clear? Think again!"

More or less the same thing persists and Maharshi says to him, "know first that 'I' and then you shall know the truth!"

This is the wonder that this incident evokes in us after so many years. Most seekers want answers to their questions which do not shake their ingrained convictions. In short, answers their 'own' 'I' prompts. Or, alternatively, they want to experience some miracle or magic. With the assumption that they will give instant freedom.

Perhaps, Bhagawan remained silent initially, and thereby gave Brunton a taste of what it is to be free from the 'I'. But then it persists. How to make functional and not a foundational entity of the Self? Bhagawan's advice is luminously clear, direct:

> "When you go back there, you shall have this peace which you now feel. But its price will be that you shall henceforth cast aside the idea that you are this body or this brain. When this peace will flow into you then you shall have to forget your own self, for you will have turned your life over to THAT!"

But, if I am not mistaken, this Brunton gets in a dream.

Should it remain a dream for us, too?

9

Bhagawan In Czechoslovakia

When a flower blossoms, the fragrance attracts many. It happens spontaneously, without any fanfare or publicity. Similar is the way in which Mahatmas attract sincere seekers; language is no barrier; distance is not an obstacle, and physically one need not crave for *darshan*. The magic works and it is futile to talk about how. For there can be no conclusive answer.

Perhaps, the sages themselves long for sincere seekers to come. Either explicitly or through some *shakti* which is beyond explanation. Sri Ramakrishna, for instance, after he emerged from his unprecedented *sadhana* and established himself in what he called *bhavamukha*, threshold of consciousness, used to go to the top of the temple and articulate his intense longing: "Where are you, my children? Come! Share the inner wealth that my Mother Bhavatarini has given me! It is just waiting for you to claim! Come soon! I am longing to see you all!"

A parallel incident happened in the case of Bhagawan. The day as usual was full of radiance with the presence of Bhagawan in his usual place in the ashram. "My mind still floats in the luminous atmosphere that Sri Ramakrishna's presence creates wherever he goes," said the Brahmo leader Pratap Chandra Majumdar. That luminosity we can easily feel in the interior of our being even today regarding Bhagawan too. It is timeless, ever-present and envelops everyone. Envelops even those who are resistant and brimming with questions. Then Bhagawan spoke:

> "Did we receive that article Dr. Radhakrishnan promised to send? You all were eager to get it. What happened?"
> "It has not been received ... yet," said the one looking after the job.
> "You wanted to print it as the very first article. Right?" asked Bhagawan.
> "Yes, Bhagawan. But so far nothing has happened and we don't know the reason. Maybe he is busy or perhaps some professional work keeps him engaged."

Bhagawan smiled and said:

> "If it is to come, it will come; otherwise, if it is destined not to come, it is equally ok. Whatever is to happen will happen. There is nothing to feel worried about... ."

The devotees knew this was the essence of Bhagawan's attitude. Even since he had arrived at Arunachala and remained as *achala*, they all knew this attitude was ingrained in him. And he impressed it on the devotees, too.

Bhagawan In Czechoslovakia

"But do you know what happened today? It is interesting in the context of that article we were talking about..." said Bhagawan.

The devotees perked their ears:

"Among the letters we received today, there was one from a distant land. Czechoslovakia," continued Bhagawan.

"Czechoslovakia?" a devotee asked.

"Yes. We have no idea who that devotee is and how he came to know about me and about this place. It's all a mystery," said Bhagawan.

Personally, I felt when I read about this incident that Bhagawan was enacting a role in his *leela*. Ramana *Leela*: the divine play of Bhagawan. When a devotee in a distant land and a different language comes to know about Bhagawan and feels spontaneously inspired to communicate his delight at this discovery, will not Bhagawan, the *sarvajna*, all knowing sage, know how the devotee came to know about him? But then Bhagawan has his own ways of unfolding a scene.

The devotees were, Bhagawan knew, eager to know more about the letter. With eyes hardly concealing his affection for them, he asked the letter to be read out. The gist was:

"My body is, in fact, at a great distance from Arunachala. But spiritually it is at Bhagawan's lotus feet. I am told that fifty years will be completed by 1st September of this year from the time young Ramana reached Tiruvannamalai. I seek your consent to celebrate the occasion here."

And the Czechoslovakian devotee closed the letter with deeply moving words:

> "I will try to celebrate the festival with an endeavour to submerge my mind in the dust of the feet of Bhagawan with limitless devotion, faith and regard and with my heart dwelling on Bhagawan's voice."

I have quoted the words almost verbatim. The language shows utmost familiarity with the idiom of devotion. Indeed, if the identity is not known, one would certainly think that it was by a Hindu devotee. "The lotus feet" is a familiar phrase, and the observation about "Bhagawan's voice" and his mind dwelling on it is something almost incredible. He never saw Bhagawan and he never heard his voice. How then, could his heart get tuned?

Obviously, there is seeing different from seeing, hearing different from hearing. They do not require the physical props. Here is, perhaps, an instance of what is called "*anahata*," the unstruck but heard sound, heard in the depths of one's contemplative awareness.

This is not so supernatural or mysterious as we are inclined to think. How does a student taking an examination listen through the ear and hear an echo of the answers? Of course, he hears his teacher first telling the answers while teaching the text. If the vibrations of an ordinary lesson in a secular context energises memory, is there a limit to vibrations – limits of time and space – to Bhagawan's auditory and visual communion with a devotee whose whole being is shot through with devotion, faith and love for him?

Bhagawan In Czechoslovakia

"You are anxiously waiting for Dr. Radhakrishna's article. But see this strange thing. Czechoslovakia and Tiruvannamalai! Can anyone even imagine not just the distance but the devotion of one who has never seen me! And yet so different from those who have seen me, heard me!" wondered Bhagawan.

These things happen. Didn't sister Devamata exclaim in awe on seeing the photograph of Sri Ramakrishna in New York Vedanta Society? She already 'saw' him in another context, not exactly conscious!

This is the power that lies in the Presence that transcends all the shackles of time, space and causation. So those of us who regret that we have not 'seen' Bhagawan, are, I think, victims of materialism. What is materialism except dogmatic reliance on matter only as real? But we find an answer if we base our enquiry on 'who am I?' with Bhagawan himself as the focus. Then:

"Who am I?" asks Bhagawan.
"You are the ocean of limitless love engulfing the entire cosmos! We are waves sometimes conscious, mostly unaware. But we are certain about one thing: your unconditional love!" we say.

10

The One Who Tried But Couldn`t Get Away!

"As I sat in his presence," a New Yorker, William S, Spaulding(Jr.,) records, "for the first time, the most powerful impression was that of what I can only call an almost palpable 'Golden radiance,' the visual effect of a tremendous spiritual force. There was an intense and subtle radiation that seemed to flow from him continuously – and once having sensed this, words, questions, techniques of meditation etc., seemed to dissolve immediately."

Intense, subtle radiation that dissolves all doubts, questions. What a Presence Bhagawan's is! But can we really give our unquestioning consent that this is true. One part of our being instantly believes it. The other slowly raises its somewhat ugly head: Is the person who recorded this free from romanticising? Can there be such phenomenon where all hurdles are brushed away?

The One Who Tried But Couldn't Get Away!

The word 'radiation' is a clue which, perhaps, explains the love of Bhagawan, its nature and effect. My mentor 'Sri Ram' once told me that (in fact, if your belief is not strained, he told me about this a day earlier to my reading the above passage) radiation and conductivity explain the nature of love. In radiation, there is no need for connectivity. We enjoy the warmth of a campfire on a winter night, the warmth of its radiation caresses us without cutting into us with its heat! Suppose, there is connectivity with live wire, it electrocutes us! In short, the love of extraordinary sages like Bhagawan is radiating love. And its radius is all-pervasive. It makes resistance crumble, reservations collapse. But all this is done softly, gently — often even without our knowing what is happening to us.

Such a phenomenon happened quite often. Bhagawan "orchestrated the scene in such a way," says Chalam, the most distinguished modern Telugu writer that "everything that needed to happen, happened automatically." True. Perhaps, one would like to substitute the word "spontaneously" with "automatically."

One of the friends of Chalam was a sceptic, a rationalist. Babas, Swamis and their ilk he avoided like plague:

"I am curious, yes. But don't ask me to believe everything he says. Not only that, don't expect me to follow the usual rituals associated with such people," he told Chalam.
"Such as?" Chalam asked.
"Prostrating, to name one. I have decided not to fall at the feet of your Swami. Certainly not," the friend replied firmly.

"Does it matter whether you touch his feet or not? He himself may not care for such things. But he has strange ways of doing precisely what makes your resistance crumble like a pack of cards," Chalam said.

Yes. This is absolutely true. Anyone who has even a grain of acquaintance with Bhagawan can vouch for what Chalam said. Bhagawan knows where to strike, where to hit: the vulnerable, the Achilles' heel, so that the resistance is gone. And the gentle stream of his compassion flows through the parched heart of the resistant person. Don't the prophets love their prodigal children more than their dutiful ones?

"So what will you do?" Chalam asked.

"Roam around! Wherever and whatever I want to see, I am free to do, I suppose!" the friend said with a sarcasm hardly concealed.

And he did exactly that. It was summer and Tiruvannamalai must have felt the heat. He roamed idly seeing things in the ashram and around — in short, without any aim or reason. Except not to break his resolve: not to go and see Bhagawan and prostrate as others do. Was it egoism? Perhaps. But the more important aspect, seems to me, is the so-called rational temper. Even today there are rationalisits who cling to their own convictions – like, as the Telugu proverb says, "the hare I caught has only three legs!"

Even when demonstrable proof stares at them in the face, they cannot suspend their self-imposed convictions. Such convictions are, in fact, convictions: getting imprisoned by themselves, even when there are definite chances of the conviction getting commuted.

Arunachala, the holy visible form of Shiva – whose call made Venkataraman, 17-year old then, run to him only to be Bhagawan Ramana later. The sheer majesty of the mountain: did it fall in the vision of this man, Chalam's friend, in his wanderings?" Did he even remotely get an inkling of the fact that Arunachala was not a hill, but the palpable, visible vibrant form of the Great God Shiva himself? If only he had a little bit of eye for such things, he would know what prison houses reason and rationality are!

We know that Bhagawan's eyes used to shed tears of joy when anything about Arunachala was read out to him. He used to go into such depths of contemplation that even the word Samadhi is inadequate to describe or evoke the impact. In fact, one of the hymns is partly evocative of this impact:

> Oh, Arunachala! As you claimed, my body and soul were yours. What else can I desire? You are both merit and demerits. Oh my life! I cannot think of these apart from you. Do as you wish, my Beloved; but grant me only everlasting love for you.

No wonder that Bhagawan saw the hill as an integral, inseparable form of Shiva himself (we feel, of Bhagawan himself).

But all this may not have registered on the one looking around the ashram and beyond. And Bhagawan now shifted the scene.

Since it was summer and very hot inside, Bhagawan's chair was placed outside. In the open, near the well, in the ashram compound. Why did Bhagawan get this done? The apparent reason is heat in the hall. But the real reason is to catch the fish roaming outside without falling into the ocean of Bhagawan's love. Bhagawan is a master angler, a wonderful fisher of men and women in his own way.

If that small boil of prejudice, born out of egoism is removed, the innate emotions will be released and the hard crust of preconceived notions broken. For that it is necessary to come face to face with each other. We know Bhagawan's Presence is irresistibly disarming. The simple reason is, his all-encompassing love for those who show the slightest interest to come to his abode, his Presence.

Miraculously, the geographical scenario did exactly what was needed. The prostration – reluctant person was exactly in that place, at the time of his wanderings, where Bhagawan sat in the chair with devotees gazing at him intently. With what curiosity they came, with what heart-rending grief they sought out Bhagawan, with what thirst for *jnana* they came to drink at the perennial fountain of his grace, who can say or guess? Whether they got what they wanted or received joyously what Bhagawan wanted to give – not what they desired but what, he thought, was desirable — this is also a moot question.

But we know for certain that this reluctant visitor felt an "irresistible" urge, an insistent desire, compelling in its strength, not just to see Bhagawan now, but do what all along he definitely decided not to. In short, instantly he fell prostrate, full length, at Bhagawan's feet! Those blessed feet which graced this earth with their holy touch out of infinite compassion to all those who are laden with the sorrow that sorrow is! He could easily have remained, shining in his own splendour, in silence and solitude. But then we had to taste his love! He allowed us to share his wealth which no currency would buy but which was easily available, freely available to all those who wish to receive and who are not reluctant to receive.

What was Bhagawan's response? When the reluctant one fell headlong at his feet, Chalam reports, "Bhagawan laughed loudly." Is it the triumphant but tender laughter of a Master Angler who landed a big fish but is reluctant to catch the bait? Who can escape Bhagawan? Provided he decides to catch!

The devotees were puzzled. They looked around. Is there anything laughable around? The usually serene, tranquil Bhagawan is not just smiling, but laughing loudly? The answer is in one of the songs that Sri Ramakrishna was fond of:

> In the world's busy market place, O Syama, Thou art flying kites!
> High up they roam on the winds of hope, held fast by maya's string.
> One of a hundred thousands of kites, at best but one or two break free.
> And Thou dost laugh and clap Thy hands, O mother, watching them!
> On favoring winds, says Ramprasad, the Kites set loose will speedily
> Be borne away to the Infinite, across the sea of the world!

Yes, the reason for Bhagawan's laughter is evident. For where will the kite – the reluctant visitor – be borne away? Except to Bhagawan himself, one of the most glorious and lovable manifestations of that Infinite? For that matter, we all will go there only whether we are reticent, reluctant or reserved, it hardly matters.

11

Where Is The 'I` To Identify A Name?

What a funny thing in retrospect! The future Bhagawan who is adored and venerated all over the globe as the exemplar of the path of Self-enquiry had to copy some lessons in a grammar book three times. Once is bad enough so far as grammar is concerned. Three times copying a lesson in *Bain's English Grammar* – perhaps a standard text in those days – was too much. The imposition was for his neglect of studies. Ever since he went beyond both death and life and experienced the state or non-state of being beyond all pairs of qualities, he found all studies painful; and, one can add, grammar lessons particularly.

Standing before the image of Mother Meenakshi, he used to shed tears of joy. His entire consciousness felt the radiation of Mother's love! In the face of that experience, will any other appear tastier? The bliss was indescribable: the bliss of the Self, *atmarama ananda*! And what is the place in such a context of, what Sri Ramakrishna called, "the plantain and rice bundling" education!

But Venkataraman was an obedient boy. He tried. Two times he copied the lesson. That was enough. He put his hand for doing it the third time and the futility of the job struck him. Perhaps, as forcibly as the "awakening" earlier. He set it aside. His natural state of meditation overwhelmed him. (What a puerile word 'meditation' is for his state!) And all along his elder brother was watching him. He noticed this brother's vagaries. Of late, he observed, something has happened to Venkataraman.

His earlier buoyancy and outgoing nature seemed to have left him. He was withdrawn, distracted; often giving the impression of staring into space! What was happening to him Nagaswami could hardly guess. It is as it should be. His perception was that Venkataraman was simply wasting his time. The appearance of meditation struck Nagaswami as, at best, shirking studies and, at worst, a huge pretence.

He now felt that the limit has been reached. Why is Venkataraman sitting like that? Isn't it time to pull him up for neglecting his studies? As an elder brother (and in the absence of a father) he felt it was his duty to do that. To call the bluff! With annoyance and sarcasm blended effectively he said, his voice instinct with the cutting edge of a rapier:

"What use is all this grammar business for such an exalted being like you!"

Though he felt the sarcasm was to awaken his brother to his vocation as a student, if one removes the sarcasm, Nagaswami was speaking the truth. Yes. For the one who taught – as no one else did, in recent history—the grammar, so to say, of self-enquiry, what were Bain's English grammar lessons? Indeed, it is only after the funeral of the linguistic grammarian that the syntax of freeing oneself from it is uncovered

> "Yes. My brother has said the right thing. Why should I live like hermit but continue to enjoy the cosiness of home and all that it indicates? My brother is speaking the truth. And I should do what he is, though ironically, suggesting."

Perhaps, this was the response of Venkataraman.

> "Didn't I feel thrilled when Arunachala was mentioned. As soon as the word fell on my ears, there was a shock of recognition I never felt before, and which never left me since."

Yes. The cards were falling for him to reach Arunachala. Shiva was making all the arrangements. Venkataraman decided to leave home instantly. No further delay. But he had a problem.

Where to get the money to reach Tiruvannamalai? Whom to ask? Can he divulge to anyone his 'plan' to leave home to reach the homeless but omnipresent Shiva in Arunachala? That was unwise. But, if the resolution is right, Nature arranges everything. We know, for example, when Sri Ramakrishna wanted to put together a small hut in Panchavati for his *sadhana,* the required materials – bamboos, thatched leaves etc., came floating down the river Ganga one day! He joyously claimed his Mother Kali's gift and got the required thing built!

Venkataraman announced:

> "I have to go to school for a class on electricity!"

He was determined, come what may to leave Madurai that very instant. The Lord, he firmly believed, would certainly look after him!

> "Since you are going to school, you may as well pay my college fee. It is due. Take five rupees from auntie and pay it!" said Nagaswami.

To reach the Lord, you require money? Do you? Yes, after all the money and prosperity bestower, Lakshmi, is herself a Goddess! And consort of Vishnu. So there is absolutely nothing wrong in using it as the right means for the right end. Venkataraman must have almost jumped with joy at this windfall.

But even here, in Venkataraman, the future Ramana Bhagawan, whom my mentor Sri Ram described as *Kaupina Dhari* but *Kaivalya Vihari*: the wearer of Loin cloth but one who roams, exultingly, in the vast, limitless expenses of the Ultimate Reality, showed his attitude of all renouncer.

> "Yes, replied Venkataraman "I will take the money, pay the fee and go to school."

But, after a quick calculation, he learnt that 3 rupees were enough for his momentous transition from home to Arunachala. Why take 5 rupees when three are enough?

But then after taking the money, he decided he should tell the truth. He wrote a letter which, it seems to me, is one of the most significant documents which he ever penned. He wrote:

> "I have set out in quest of my Father in accordance with his command. It is on a virtuous enterprise that this one

has embarked, therefore, let none grieve over this act and let no money be spent in search of this. Your college fees have not been paid. Two rupees are enclosed herewith...."

This is, as we noted, a remarkable letter in many ways. The first thing which strikes us is the absence of the *Advaita Vedanta Idiom*! Venkataraman uses, instead, the idiom of *Bhakti*, devotion. He was setting out to discover his Father!

But is there any difference between *Bhakti* and *Jnana*? Are they not identical? We know that Bhagawan later said categorically:

> "Jnana Marga and Bhakti Marga are one and the same. Self-surrender leads to realization just as inquiry does. Complete self-surrender means, you have no further thought of 'I'. Then all your predispositions (Samskaras) are washed away and you are free. You should not continue as a separate entity at the end of either course."

Not only Bhagawan Ramana affirmed the identity of both, he also affirmed that he himself set out in quest of the Father. The added revelation "in accordance with his command" is much more fascinating.

We know that one of the books which Venkataraman found enthralling was *Periya Puranam*. It is full of narratives of Tamil Saivaite saints. There are many stories which portray sages and saints who left everything once the call of Shiva came. It is in that tradition that, perhaps, one has to place "the command of the Father" which eventually "transformed" Venkataraman into Bhagawan Ramana, in this context.

Doesn't this have further significance? Many admirers and devotees of Bhagawan naturally assume he is the most outstanding figure in Jnana Marga. Indeed, his classic "*Who Am I?*" is the most crucial exposition of the path of self-inquiry. But, even in that precious gem of a book, Bhagawan says, "through meditation on forms of God and through repetition of mantras, the mind becomes one-pointed." Yet, at the same time, he affirms, "what exists in truth is the Self alone. The world, the individual soul and God are appearances in it...."

Moreover, there is also something much more revealing. He never uses the word "I". "Enterprise this one embarked.... Let no money be spent in this...." The most profound hint is the total absence of signature. Only three or four dots. No identity with Venkataraman!

One finds this, to say the least, staggering. There is, even at that point of embarking on the Great journey, nothing of the awareness of Name and Form in Bhagawan. Total undifferentiated awareness that simply Is! Therefore, the Father who commanded him does not cease to exist. In that ocean of cosmic consciousness, forms rise, dissolve, rise again – what Sri Ramakrishna experienced along with his profound devotion to Mother Bhavatarini.

One does not know whether Bhagawan "signed" his name at any stage, but we have this fascinating incident narrated by Arthur Osborne: when a Chinese visitor was given a copy of "*Who am I?*", he persisted in Bhagawan autographing it. "Bhagawan finally took it," says Osborne, "and wrote in it the Sanskrit symbol for Om, the sacred monosyllable representing the Primordial sound underlying all creation."

There is an interesting parallel here. The 17-year old refused to affix his signature. Now he simply writes Om. Most appropriate because, Om is neither a word nor a name. It is "the sound of the Soundless Absolute." And "this syllable is the whole world..... the past, the present and the future – everything is but the sound Om." And whatever else that transcends time – that too, is but the sound Om." Moreover, Om, consisting of four parts (with the *anuswara*), points to the four states of consciousness, *Jagrat, swapna, sushupti, and turiya.*

Turiya is the transcendental Self beyond the mind. Bhagawan himself affirmed: "Omkara" is Ishwara, Ishwara is Omkara. That means omkara itself is the swarupam (the real Self). Some say that the swarupam itself is omkara, some say it is Ishwara, some say it is Jesus, some say it is Allah. Whatever name is given, the thing there is only one."

Look at the profundity of the movement from absence of signature to the primal sound Om. No wonder that once Venkataraman reached Arunachala, the experience of this nature continued. He was totally oblivious to everything – Unaware of anything. It was a state of timeless ananda, and who would like to come back to anything temporal?

But he did. For our sake, for gently leading, whoever needs, along the Path, which is no path at all. "There will come a time," Bhagawan said, "when one will have to forget all that one has learned."

We are willing to forget, may one add, all that we have learned. But is it possible to forget Bhagawan? Try and you will find what a formidable job it is!

12

To Be Angry Or Not? That`s The Question

Many of us feel that negative emotions like anger are to be got rid of. We hear again and again about the power of positive thinking. Psychologists constantly exhort us to get rid of all these negatives so that our creativity flowers without any block. This kind of thought influences us very much and we try to control our negative emotions. But the question is, do we really control them or suppress them? Suppress because religious scriptures generally declare such negatives to be undesirable. They, therefore, fester inside.

> "Bhagawan! I have a recurring problem," said a devotee who was, by his appearance, highly disturbed.
> "All of us have problems. You are not alone. Look at this ashrama. Its maintenance involves many problems. Leave it there. Tell me, what is your problem?" replied Bhagawan.

On his face appeared a fleeting, hardly noticeable, feeling of being amused. Not exactly amused, but understanding the recurrence of problems and their inevitability, he felt that there is no need to feel agitated.

> "I get angry many times. In spite of trying my best, I am not able to control this emotion. I know I should not entertain anger but I do. I am helpless and frequently a victim of this emotion," the young man plaintively told Bhagawan. His tone expressed the sorrow he felt at his repeated failure.

We all feel this emotion, without doubt. But we also feel, almost always, that we should get rid of this if we wish to grow "spiritually." In Bhagawan's idiom, "to know who we are?"

We also experience this emotion so spontaneously that no amount of introspective wisdom will help us. We burst into anger like petrol coming close to a matchstick. It is inflammable stuff. But is it so inflammable? We wonder whether Bhagawan himself was not angry at any time. At least one context we can recall. When those who "looked after him", his attendants, became somewhat lax, he scolded them saying that in the presence of the public they were all attention but, often, when no one was around they were evidently lax in doing what he wanted them to.

Bhagawan heard, in this 'case', the devotee repeatedly saying that he was being abused and asked him what he should do. How he should respond. Bhagawan heard, but kept silent. No response at all. The devotee repeatedly presented his case to Bhagawan. Indeed, he vociferously complained, but Bhagawan kept mum. The devotee's patience was, obviously, wafer thin. He could hardly exercise further restraint. One can easily imagine his predicament. And he told Bhagawan what he felt straightaway.

"Unnecessarily, without any reason, I am abused. I loose my patience and get angry. It is impossible to control it."

Here is the actual demonstration of annoyance, if not anger, directed at or issuing from Bhagawan's silence, without reacting to what he said. Isn't Bhagawan's response "cool" in spite of the devotees repeated appeals to him to show him some way of controlling his anger.

One is amused. A person who could not contain his annoyance even with Bhagawan, in spite of repeated and varied complaints of his anger, is bound to be predictably angry at the slightest stimulus.

Did Bhagawan remain irresponsive to see that his anger found a tangible context for coming out so that one can gauge its intensity? To be assured that his anger was really severe, intense.

"What shall I do Bhagawan?" the devotee asked helplessly.

Now Bhagawan knew the time is right and ripe. He laughed and said:

"You too join the one who abuses you and abuse yourself! That's the way to control it!"

The devotees, in the hall where Bhagawan sat, laughed. Perhaps, the devotee who was really bothered by his anger, may not have found anything laughable. Admittedly what Bhagawan said was inexplicable:

"I should abuse myself! Isn't it very helpful?" he said, with some intended irony.

"Yes it is helpful. Indeed, it is very helpful," said Bhagawan and explained why he made such a suggestion.

"When they abuse, what those people are abusing is the body. Don't you agree? Can you find a greater enemy than this body? It is the repository of anger and all other feelings. Therefore, to hate it is necessary – hate ourselves, and, when such abuse is faced it is a wake-up call. They are alerting us to our nature. Therefore, join the ones who abuse you!"

Bhagawan explained thus. And added the reason for the apparently puzzling abuse:

"What is the use of counter-abuse? In fact, people who abuse us are our friends. You should view them as such. People who praise us, in fact, are deceiving us! They don't mean what they say. They are taking you for a ride," explained Bhagawan.

Bhagawan is not only a *jnani*, but also one who knew the, alas, neglected art of getting along with all kinds of people. In short, we require a lot of worldly wisdom.

But, then, Ramana Swami does not give the same advice, blanket-wise, to all. And, often, he hides his subtle suggestion in a tissue of enjoyable humor. Humor is caught, but often, the suggestion is lost. Even sensing humor is itself a potentially spiritual act. Sri Ramakrishna gave a description of Cosmic Humor enjoyed by God: "God laughs on two occasions. One is when two brothers quarrel about division of land: One says, 'so much is mine!' and the other equally vehemently asserts, 'this much is mine! You don't intrude!' God laughs at this and says to himself: 'the entire cosmos is mine! And they wrangle an infinite part of it as theirs! What fun!' Similarly when a doctor assures a patient: 'Don't worry, dear! However chronic your disease is, I shall cure it! God laughs again: 'the fellow is fated to die. And the doctor, poor fellow, assures the patient that he will cure him!' Now look at this laughable incident, again, about anger.

> "My senses are playing tricks, Bhagawan! I try desperately, but I am nowhere near controlling them, please cure me!" said a young devotee.
> "Everything is due to the mind. Set it right and there won't be any problem, any problem," Bhagawan said.
> "I am particularly worried about my anger. I try to control it. It boomerangs, what should I do?"

Like a trigger of instruction came Bhagawan's answer:

> "Then get angry with anger, that's the cure for all."

"All people in the hall burst out laughing," says Suri Nagamma who reports the incident. They laughed yes but did they learn what it meant? In fact, we who come later and do not have access, do we learn? Decode at least partially what Bhagawan meant? Nagamma interprets it thus: "A person who gets angry with everything in the world, if only he introspects and enquires why does he not get angry with his anger itself, will he not really overcome all anger?"

Yes, he or she will. The only condition is whether anger is justified or not. In some contexts anger is a weakness, a defect in character, often destructive. In another, anger is warranted if the context calls for it. Even then the basic idea is that only if one is capable of anger, then only can its use to be decided.

Is this a bit abstract? Look at Sri Ramakrishna's advice to two of his disciples. The context was the same. Once a disciple of the Master, travelling by a boat from Calcutta to Dakshineswar, heard a fellow abusing his Master. The disciple burst into a rage and threatened to drown the entire boat if the fellow did not stop. He came and reported the incident to the Master, expecting him to praise his devotion to the guru. Instead, the Master spoke sharply: "Does it matter? Dogs bark while the elephant moves on!"

The response of another disciple was sharply in contrast: he found another fellow traveller doing the same thing speaking with derision and disrespect about the Master. The disciple sat calmly thinking to himself: "Poor fellow! What does this guy know about our Master! We should pity him, pity such people." And dutifully told the Master about this. The Master took him to task: "Fie on you! What kind of disciple are you? Your guru is called bad names and you sit quietly. Is this the respect you have for your guru?" The disciple was taken aback! So should he have been angry?

We are also taken aback. Should we or should we not be angry? Bhagawan would say, enquire who is this 'I' who gets angry? Who is the 'other' who called forth this anger? Such a *vichara* ultimately is psychological. It digs deep into the psyche with all its strengths and weaknesses so that we don't misperceive *tamas* for *sattva* or *rajas* for *tamas*.

Anger in itself is tremendous energy. It is, in Gandhiji's coining Satyagraha, "Satya Agraha" – anger that is based on Knowing what is the truth of *iccha*, *jnana* and *kriya* saktis – will, cognition and action.

Am I complicating matters and you resent my attempt at making simple things abstract? Then this itself is a context to check whether you should be angry at what I did or tried to do here!

13

Peace Of Bliss

All that we think, feel, and out of that thinking and feeling, do is generally to gain one thing: Happiness. We want to be happy and devoid of sorrow. That is, we want happiness and the cessation of sorrow: *sukha prapti* and *dukha nivritti*. But then what is happiness? Can it be completely autonomous without the slightest trace of sorrow?

First let us look at one context in which Bhagawan was asked a question, which all of us feel tempted to ask:

> "Does the sage use occult powers for making others realize the Self or is the mere fact of his Self-realization enough for it?"

Very pointed question and it is precisely what almost all of us nurture and nourish in some remote corner of our mind: Can't Bhagawan give Self-realization as a means to happiness just like that? On a plate?

In other words, we want to be happy and if Self-realization is a means to that end why can't we have it like something which we buy for money? Look at the second part of the question: "is the mere fact of his Self-realization enough for it?" In other words, happiness is primary. But does Self-realization include happiness? Is it meant to make enough of happiness available?

But what is happiness? Bhagawan says that one should think about happiness in the context of "bliss"; one's very nature is blissful. Then why do we crave for happiness? Moreover, is 'Bliss' (with a capital 'B') different from happiness? Says Bhagawan:

> "Being of the nature of Bliss, why does one continue to crave for happiness? To be rid of that craving is itself salvation. The Scripture says, 'You are That'. The imparting of that knowledge is their purpose. The realization must be by your finding out who you are and abiding as That, i.e., your Self."

Similarly, we not only want happiness but we want its "permanency" says Bhagawan:

> "The desire for permanency of happiness and peace suggests permanency in his own nature. Therefore, he seeks to find his own nature, i.e., his Self. That found, all is found.

Moreover, why this craving? Bhagawan says, this is so to say, a shadow of the Bliss which is our real nature. This means there is no need for seeking it. Does anyone try to seek the spectacles which rest on one's own nose? 'There is no happiness' is only a thought. Elaborating this, Bhagawan says:

The Self is bliss, pure and simple. You are the Self. So you cannot be but bliss; being so, you cannot say there is no happiness. That which says so cannot be the Self; it is the non-Self and must be got rid of in order to realize the bliss of the Self.

So happiness does not exist in reality. It is absent and we must look for it as part of the fabric of *maya* or cosmic illusion. We crave for it for the simple reason that as a thought it does exist: happiness is a thought and everything connected with its absence or presence is also a thought. Once we are convinced it is a thought, why not go in for that *thing* which is not a thought or a realization but is our intrinsic, inalienable nature itself? Once we know it is our nature, our *sahaja sthithi*, does anyone hug the thought of happiness and not its relief? As Sri Ramakrishna asks: "If you fold and squeeze a *panchangam*, an almanac, will you get rain? It predicts the quantum of rain for the year but is not rain itself!"

Bhagawan gives the analogy of a headache:

"The desire for happiness (*sukha prema*) is a proof of ever-existing happiness of the Self. Otherwise, how can desire for it arise in you? If headaches were natural for human beings, no one would try to get rid of it. But everyone who has a headache tries to get rid of it, because he has known a time when he had no headache. He desires only that which is natural to him. So, he too desires happiness because it is natural to him. Because it is natural, it is not acquired. Man's attempt can only be to get rid of misery. If that is done, the ever-present bliss is felt."

Happiness is not that but misery. For the simple reason, that it is not "ever-present" or perennial. In other words, since happiness is only a thought it breeds misery. Since happiness as a thought is the shadow and not the substance, why not claim the substance which is our real, natural state?

We now have an extension of the quest for happiness. The quest is not necessary at all, it is the extension. Since we feel miserable because we are not happy, if we get rid of misery happiness results is the assumption. Is this true? Absence of misery is happiness is a myth until we realize that happiness of any sort is misery because it goes with misery. In short, happiness and misery are inalienable twins. If we get some happiness, we realize that in its wake misery comes along. Bhagawan knew that "happiness", "bliss", etc., are heavily loaded words which have their own linguistic connotations. For instance, *ananda* is not just happiness but Bliss. And *sukha*, as far as I know, cannot be wholly happiness, it is its sensuous *avatar*. This, it seems to me, is the reason for Bhagawan using another related word, "Pleasure":

> Happiness mixed with misery is only misery. When misery is eliminated then the ever-present bliss is said to be gained. Pleasure which ends in pain is misery.

It is this pleasure that, adds Bhagawan, "man wants to eschew," and he talks of three kinds of pleasures. "Pleasures are *priya, moda* and *pramoda*. When a desired object is near at hand, there arises *priya*; when it is taken possession of, *moda* arises; when it is being enjoyed, *pramoda* prevails."

Happiness and pleasure are not *ananda*, our natural state of Bliss. The test whether it is ananda or not lies in the fact that "*ananda*" generates "peace." Happiness and pleasure engender restlessness and craving. In other words, *Nisananda* goes beyond happiness and pleasure. One may be happy but not at "peace" with himself, unless he realizes the fact that happiness is born out of peace and not from the thought of happiness which leads to its quest. Now look at the interlocking system of happiness and peace, as Bhagawan describes it:

> What is the highest benefit that can be conferred on others? It is happiness. Happiness is born of peace. Peace can reign only when there is no disturbance. Disturbance is due to thoughts arising in the mind. When the mind itself is absent, there will be perfect Peace. Unless a person has annihilated his mind, he cannot gain peace and be happy. Unless he himself is happy, he cannot confer happiness on others.

All this is an intricate chain, a "network," so to say, of the "who am I?" inquiry.

When the mind is free of thought, it becomes absent and there is, therefore no disturbance; misery ceases and peace descends. And the peace confers happiness. Only such a happy person can confer happiness on another.

Forget the equation. It does not matter. Instead don't we have irrefutable proof that this happiness and joy born out of *Poorna Santi,* Perfect Peace that Bhagawan radiated in his person. For instance, Swami Ramdas, Head, coincidentally of Anandashram, Kanhangad records that:

"The Maharshi turned his beautiful eyes towards Ramdas and looked intently for a few minutes into his eyes, as though he was pouring into Ramdas his blessings through those orbs. Then he shook his head as if to say he has been blessed. A thrill of inexpressible joy coursed through the frame of Ramdas, his whole body quivering like a leaf in the breeze."

This is, surely, what Bhagawan called transmission of happiness born out of perfect peace. And Viswanatha Swami, who observed Bhagawan closely, describes, echoes almost, Bhagawan's words quoted above: "In his presence, the unique bliss of peace was directly experienced."

14

You Also Don`t Take

One of the qualities of Bhagawan's nature, as of all of his stature, is to seize every context for illuminating facets of *sadhana* or the quest for the Truth. For such people there is no distinction between an apparently secular context and a 'spiritual' insight. Or, rather, there is a natural link between the two. Bhagawan saw beyond the context to unlock a text of immense significance for inner life.

> "Why are you demanding more fare than what is usual? You are asking for double the amount. Are you such a deceitful fellow that you are exploiting this man who came from the north to have darshan of Bhagawan?" Krishanaswami, a follower of Bhagawan, almost shouted at the jutkawalla.

The horse drawn carriage was near the ashram and Krishnaswami saw from a distance that something wrong was going on. When he rushed there the devotee from the north asked him what the usual fare from the railway station to the ashram was. When Krishnaswami told him and heard the fare the driver of the Jutka was demanding, he was furious.

> "Sir! You don't interfere. It is our business; we have to make a living. And I haven't asked much," rejoined the jutkawallah.
> "It is double the amount. I won't allow this outright deception," shouted Krishnaswami.

The devotee from the north was confused and obviously helpless. He didn't know whether he should pay it off and be done with it. He had come to have *darshan* of the Swami, not get bogged down because of a difference in fare.

> "Who are you, Sir, to allow it or not? You have nothing to do with my fare. It is between me and that saab who came in my vehicle," said the jutkawallah, in a belligerent tone.

The north-Indian devotee realized that he was wasting his time. He was eager to have *darshan* of Bhagawan and the fare business was delaying the purpose for which he had come all the way from the north.

> "Don't bother, Sir," the pilgrim told Krishnaswami. "A few rupees extra do not matter. He is not listening to you at all. Let him go," the devotee told Krishnaswami and paid off whatever the 'fellow' asked.
> "How stubborn this fellow is! He didn't listen to a word of what I was saying," said Krishnaswami.

This kind of fleecing a pilgrim mercilessly is very common. Unless you know the place quite well, you won't be able to avoid the almost universal cheating in religious places. Just a simple clue that you are a stranger to the place is enough, and they take the ride out of you! They won't listen to anything you say. They will stubbornly take their pound of flesh.

Krishnaswami came back, furious with the jutka "fellow." He went straight to Bhagawan. He must let Bhagawan know everything and he was sure that Bhagawan would support him. Not the driver.

> "Bhagawan! You know how stubborn that fellow was. He wanted from a devotee who came to see you from the north, double the fare from the railway station to the ashram. He didn't listen to my words at all!" Krishnaswami told Bhagawan.

Even as Krishnaswami was telling this, a smile started appearing on Bhagawan's radiant face. Doesn't he know what had happened? Straight he asked, laughing in that gentle way which takes away the sting from the unpleasant truth:

> "As if you listen to my words! Do you really follow what I tell you to do? For instance, I look upon all as equal. In my grammar, there are no degrees of comparison, and what do you do? You make me special and serve dishes prepared with ghee, and those perfumed with oil you give to those who come to see me? How many times have I told you not to serve me anything special? That everything should be given to everyone without any distinction. Don't you know it is against the practice! But do you follow?"

Krishnaswami, obviously, was taken aback. Bhagawan was smiling all through. But what he was saying is the exact truth. We find his teachings fascinating, but it is so difficult to follow.

We listen but, by and large, do not learn. But Bhagawan never leaves us. He follows us, gently, but persistently driving home the truths until they become instinctive acts.

15

When 'I` Enters, Bhagawan Exits

When the great scholar Ganapati Muni saw Ramana Maharshi, then known as "Brahmana Swami", for the first time, he expressed and evoked his impression thus:

> A sage in silence I saw for the first time; His face brimming with inner power; Unique and different was he; To the sage I bowed with all respect and uplifted thoughts.

He was obviously deeply impressed. He knew that here was no mere scholar or a saint. He was, "unique and different." And when he saw him again (on 18.11.1907) his perception got transformed and he knew that he had met, at last, his Guru who would free him from the knots of scholarship. He wrote about this to his "close disciples":

> " I have found a Guru in a Swami who lives in Arunachala and is referred to by the people as Brahmana Swami. He is a great seer, repository of unstinted virtues. He is a sage who deserves to be addressed by the venerable title

Bhagawan. I have named him as 'Ramana', both the sound and sense of which is attractive, in addition to being brief. It is my intention that the sage be referred to by this name by all of you henceforward."

And so the Brahmana Swami was henceforward known as Bhagawan Ramana Maharshi. Countless seekers from almost all over the world came to have his *darshan* and be blessed.

They were enthralled by his simplicity, transparency and above all quite often by his silence more than by his speech. But the most amusing thing was, in this case, an incident in which though they saw him, recognition eluded them.

Near the Virupaksha cave on the Arunachala Hill associated with Bhagawan, the sage himself built a platform for the convenience of visitors to sit on. It was in that situation that a stranger came to see Bhagawan.

Bhagawan was doing something which one generally does not associate with such exalted ones. He placed some stones in their right order. Then he kneaded some mud and was engrossed, obviously, in building the platform.

For Bhagawan no work was inferior or trivial. Whether it is cutting vegetables in the kitchen or pounding rice for idli, or looking after the cow Lakshmi or other animals, it had to be done with *sraddha*. The same *sraddha* we show in temples, in worship.

An absolute stranger approached Bhagawan, perhaps, covered with mud! and asked him:

"They told me that a Swami lives here. Where is the Swami?"

Yes, where is he? The answer would be: "Where is he not?" Leave that. There was no one else around. Couldn't he guess or at least have a doubt that the one he saw could be the very Swami he came all the way to see? Isn't it possible to guess, on our part, that the stranger came out of some curiosity and not any genuine urge? " Why not see him. Some merit might accrue. What do we lose by seeing?"—this must have been what the stranger thought and came up to see the Swami.

"Swami has gone out somewhere," said Bhagawan.
"Any idea when he will be back?" the stranger asked.
"I don't know," Bhagawan said, and added, " it might be a long time."

What an amusing conversation!

It reveals the thick veil of "maya" with which Bhagawan could wrap himself up. One who gave *darshan* to anyone, at any time, denied it in this case. In the first attempt, let us add.

For, we do not know how and why Bhagawan acts in the way he does. It turned out, later, that Bhagawan delayed, as it were, and not denied darshan to this stranger. And it happened in this way.

The stranger was walking down from the Virupaksha cave; Echamma was coming up with food for Bhagawan. She questioned him, and found out that he had gone to see the Swami, but couldn't find him. So he was going back.

"That cannot be," exclaimed Echamma, "I am taking food for the Swami. He must be there. Come with me. I will show him."

They went up. Echamma placed the food inside the cave and showing Bhagawan, she prostrated to him and said:

"This is the Swami. I told you, he will certainly be there. Here he is!"

The stranger was, to say the least, stupefied. How can that be? He was the same person whom he had asked. But he quickly recovered his wits and prostrated to Bhagawan. Then he told Echamma:

"He is the same person whom I asked about the Swami and he told me he has gone somewhere. He didn't even tell me when he would come back. What a strange thing!"
So saying, the stranger prostrated to Bhagawan and left.

Echamma was intrigued. Why did the Swami say that he was not there? Why did he mislead the poor fellow who had come all the way up to see him? She took courage into her hands and asked the Swami:

"Poor fellow! He was so eager to see you. It is lucky that I saw him. Otherwise, he would have gone back without your darshan!"

Bhagawan smiled but gave a characteristically revealing reply:

"What do you think I should do? Should I wear a locket or some such thing and advertise myself? How can I do that?"

Similar was another incident. The only difference was they had already had *darshan* of the Maharshi. Even then, Bhagawan was successful in eluding them.

There were two or three people rather devotees. They decided to do *parikrama* of the Arunachala Hill. They did accordingly and then while coming down, they reached the ashram for Bhagawan's darshan. They couldn't find him anywhere; he was not to be seen in his usual places—the couch, etc.

> "Where do you think Bhagawan could be?" asked one of them. "Perhaps, he is in the kitchen. You know that he frequently goes to assist in cooking. I am sure we can find him there."

They went accordingly into the kitchen to find Bhagawan, and what he was doing there, he himself told the devotees later. In her *Letters* (which is one of the most precious and extremely fascinating collection about Bhagawan), Suri Nagamma recoded it thus:

> "They were people," said Bhagawan, "who frequently visited the Ashram; what has that got to do with it? My head was wholly covered with a bedsheet and I was cutting vegetables, my face was not visible. 'Sir, Swami is not on the couch, where is he?' they asked me. I replied saying that he had just gone out and would be back in a little while."

They all went away. Ostensibly to continue their going round the hill, which they had interrupted to have Bhagawan's *darshan*. When somebody asked Bhagawan why he did such a thing, he replied:

"What else to do? ... was I to tell them that I was the Swami," said Bhagawan and added, "such incidents happen quite a number of times."

Anonymity, the shunning of any kind of attention focused on him, was always Bhagawan's hallmark. But there is also another aspect: Couldn't these two or three persons recognize his voice at least? Not only that, the Swami was the tangible form of Arunachala himself, the Great Shiva, the Lord of Destruction. But then few recognized and fewer kept that recognition steady, like an inextinguishable flame. Recognition and retention, in this regard, depend upon the intensity of aspiration, the burning desire to know oneself. To know 'who I am?' Indeed "many are called, but few are chosen."

It is extremely fascinating that such an incident happened in the case of Sri Ramakrishna, also.

One day he was strolling on the banks of the Ganges flowing by the Dakshineswar temple. Paramahamsa was enjoying the cool breeze in the evening time. At that point, he saw a lady getting down a boat docked to the Dakshineswar ghat. She approached him and asked:

> "Sir, I heard that the great saint Sri Ramakrishna lives here. It is such a big campus. Can you tell me where can I find him?"
> "I also heard about him. But I, too, do not know where he is. He must be somewhere around. Tell me if you find him," the Paramahamsa said.

The lady went all over the place. She could, naturally, find him nowhere. She came back fuming with anger and told the Master.

> "I searched and searched. He is nowhere. Unnecessarily I spent money on the boat fare. I shouldn't have bothered," she almost shouted in anger.
> "See! The boat there is ready to leave. Miss it and you won't have another for another hour," said Sri Ramakrishna.
> The lady hurried.

What is the reason for Bhagawan behaving in such a way? He himself gave the reason:

> "Rangan! You and others talk about me to your friends and acquaintances. And they come here enthusiastically. They see me sitting in a corner.
> I am immersed in silence. They say to themselves, "is this all?" and they leave us as they came. Not just leave but often they blame me."

And Rangan agrees and extends what Bhagawan said:

> Covering the curry and then putting the lid on the mind. "As a result of the solid sense, the thick crust of 'I' and 'mine', even when they see you, Bhagawan, they are unable to recognize who you are!"

Yes that is the reason for what happened in the incidents we narrated here. As my mentor, Sri Ram, puts it "when 'I' enters, ' why should 'I' be there,' says God and moves away!"

16

Cover The Curry, Put The Lid On The Mind

"Bhagawan's form, words and presence," says Varanasi Subbalakshmamma, a devotee of Bhagawan, "changed according to the reception level and the state of consciousness of those who came to have his darshan." Thus, "he was a child to children, a householder to householders, a Master to *Vedantins* and a woman to women and the Supreme Lord, Parameshwara, himself to Yogis. He used to assume and tune with their condition, their level and capture and hold their minds."

Nowhere was this more evident than in the kitchen. Bhagawan, in the kitchen, appeared to be exceptionally at home, full of fun and yet absolutely alert to what was being cooked. Subbalakshmamma rightly notes that "not only did he speak to us through words about Vedantic truths, but also in every small job—cutting the vegetables, grinding the flour, cooking various dishes for all—he used to instruct us in marvelous ways. "Who can know (fully) how he changed our very natures?" she adds.

One wonders how the kitchen was converted into a Gurukula. Based on even the various dishes getting prepared, he taught them subtle spiritual truths in the very process of cooking. Perhaps he wanted to train them in the processes of cooking worldliness, even when living in the world. If we decode this, we can say that he wanted to purify the *annamaya kosha*, the food sheath of consciousness. This sheath makes us sustain our body and our physical strength and alertness, so that the healthy body helps in the energising the other sheath such as the mental, the intellectual, the joyful, the spiritual, etc.

No wonder that Subbalakshmamma, one of the women helping in the kitchen, described Bhagawan's Presence in the kitchen as "Kitchen Sadhana" and declared unambiguously:

> "That state which the yogis try to achieve in and through severe sadhana, Maharshi gave us in our daily household and kitchen work, and made us emerge successful." Capable of absorbing the spiritual truths.

In fact, what he only occasionally told the gatherings in the main hall of the Ashram where he sat, he told demonstrably in the kitchen. Many truths emerged in the very context of cooking. An outstanding Vedantic truth which emerged was the parallel, indeed, the interconnection, between the mind and the "methodology" of cooking. Once when there was pressure in a vessel wherein a curry was being cooked, he made the cooks present observe it and said:

> "You have to cover the curry. Only then the vapour subsides. Then it gets cooked and becomes edible."

The way he looked at those who were present there, says Sampoornamma, was meant to reveal the inner truth that, "if you put the lid on the mind the inner tendencies subside. The person becomes a *Jnani* and is fit to merge in *Ishwara.*" In short, he suggested states of consciousness and their transformation as parallel to the various stages of cooking and eating.

Analogous was the way in which he used to taste a dish before it was declared ready for serving to others. We get the impression that he was fastidious about the taste, the freshness, etc. But implicit here is the most important dimension, an inestimable blessing. All those who were being served, implicitly believed that he was Arunachala Ishwara himself. Therefore, when he tasted the dishes, it was an act of not only sanctifying the food, a sacrament in itself, but also transforming every item, every grain into sacred Prasad offered to the living Ishwara! We can only guess the tremendous changes it brought about in the inner being of all those who took the prasad! Of course, as Annamalai Swami, a "kitchen assistant," himself says, that since Bhagawan was the first to arrive in the kitchen very early in the morning, it was he who lighted the fire.

"Lighted the fire" masks the enormous significance of fire in igniting inner consciousness. It is applied to hunger also; we call it *Jatharagni*, the fire of hunger which makes the food not only enormously tasty but also digests the food taken in. Similarly, we have *Jnagni* the fire of knowledge, of wisdom which burns to ashes all ignorance and delusion! And who can ignite these fires in a blazing way other than Bhagawan himself?

Bhagawan looked upon everything, literally every part of a vegetable etc., as capable of being recycled into an exceptionally tasty dish. "All these things," he affirmed, "are God's gifts, his creation. Even what appears a small, trivial thing should not be wasted. It is useful to somebody or the other. It is good to keep it." Even the skin of bitter gourds was expertly recycled, so that they became uncannily tasty. Indeed, he "detested" waste of any kind.

Lessons in curbing the ego formed an important unit of the "Kitchen syllabus". Lessons in curbing the ego were ingeniously but compassionately taught. For instance, when Shantamma sent, hesitantly, a message to Bhagawan that because of the kitchen work she suffered from bodily pain, Bhagawan hit the nail on the head:

> "Shantamma is doing all that out of a sense of the ego. Ask her to get rid of the sense of 'doership' and thereby, of her false sense of sole responsibility; she is complaining only to get noticed by people that she is working! That should cease and there won't be any problem."

One can surely find Maharshi's own way of telling what, somewhat pontifically, is called, "*Karma yoga.*" Any work becomes a joy and manifests untiring energy once the sense of "I am doing" ceases. Work, done in such a way, is a source of energizing the body and activating the mind.

Never did Bhagawan make any distinction between one and the other. All are the same. His view can be summed up by saying: "Either all are realized beings, indeed Gods, or no one is." This principle he followed without exception, without conceding any compelling context. This was evident in the way he insisted on everyone being served any dish equally without any distinction. When devotees tried to serve him more or give him dishes specially made with ghee, he would straightaway reprimand them. Until everyone was served the same, he refused to eat. As devotees testify in kitchen chronicles, he was inflexible in this aspect. And, out of misguided devotion, if any person tried to give him what he thought good for his health, he would say:

> "The tonics and vitamins you want to give me are needed more by those who labour throughout the day. I do nothing except sit here and occasionally talk, if I feel fine. Give all those things to them, they need to maintain their health carefully to serve!"

Even as Bhagawan meticulously observed such principles, he also went a step further which is nothing short of radicalism. When some woman worker stopped entering the kitchen because of monthly period, Bhagawan pointed out that this is basically a physiological aspect. It has nothing to do with defilement or absence of purity and he asked that woman to continue her routine work!

Sampurnamma, a kitchen worker, says, "Bhagawan used cooking to teach us religion and philosophy." True, but it was a wooly kind of religion and philosophy. It was cooking to change the uncooked "unripe" ego into a "ripe" one. The result was a manifestation of the inherent potential.

17

"I Will Sit On The Rock Brushing My Teeth!"

Few can understand the ways of a *Jnani*, an enlightened one. Fewer those of a person like Bhagawan Ramana. He was not a mere enlightened one. He radiated not so much enlightenment as incredible love and concern and care for anyone who had faith in him. Even, I feel, faith is not necessary. If you simply show an iota, a grain of love for him, he comes running, as it were. Didn't Sri Ramakrishna take tremendous trouble to visit his devotees? This is because such beings require only some potential warmth of affection. They will go and ignite it further, so that it becomes a blazing fire of awareness.

Look at such an incident.

"Why did you not come to see me yesterday, amma?" Bhagawan asked the old woman standing before him.

Her wrinkled body never masked her glow of reverence coupled with adoration for this Mouna Swami. There was something unearthly in her eyes—old eyes, yet eyes glowing with affection for Bhagawan. One sees such manifest feeling rarely. I mean the unmistakable light of total surrender. No wonder she took a vow that she would not eat anything in the morning without the darshan of Bhagawan.

Those were the days when Bhagawan lived at Skandasramam, on the Arunachala hill and there were few visitors. And those who came to have his darshan were, I felt, free from the questioning seekers who thronged to him later.

This lady was alone. There was a group of quite a few devotees, aged mostly, who trudged all the way up the holy hill to Skandasramam to have the darshan of Bhagawan. It was not an easy climb, certainly not for the old lady and others of comparable age. The path was uneven and going up it was quite a strain for the old. Yet they were a determined lot.

But then age catches up. The limbs are not firm. Even walking on the ground was an ordeal for such people. For this lady especially for a valid reason.

"Bhagawan, you are omniscient. Don't you know why I couldn't come?" asked the lady.

Bhagawan smiled:

"Now you are talking about something which I don't have. All knowing? Omniscient? I have nothing of that sort. I don't have any siddhis. Why should I have? Love for my Arunachala Shiva swallowed everything else, engulfed everything else. Nothing remains except that love. So you have to tell me, amma, why I didn't see you yesterday. Were you sick?"

"I Will Sit On The Rock Brushing My Teeth!"

And he smiled again. Come to think of it what a smile Bhagawan had! A visitor from California recalled her impression:

> "When (Bhagawan) smiled it was as though the gates of heaven were thrown open. I have never seen eyes more alight with Divine Illumination—they shine like stars."

And another "foreign" devotee, Chadwick reports:

> "His face wreathed in the most lovely of smiles, and an expression of serenity and beauty on it which is impossible to describe, or even believe unless you have seen it yourself …."

That is the effulgence of Bhagawan's smile. One can only add, one need not see it physically; Even a photo is enough to get a feel, a real warmth, that suffuses Bhagawan's smile. No poet, however gifted can versify its charm, its vitality, its sheer magic—I mean, the magic of the smile. If I am pardoned, one sees such a smile, easily comparable to that of Bhagawan, on the face of Sri Ramakrishna. The only difference is, in the luminous photo which framed him in Samadhi—the eyes are closed. Those of Bhagawan are open.

When he smiled at the old lady, one can imagine it, the smile of an eternal child of Arunachala Shiva! Basking in the glory and grandeur of His abode, Arunachala.

> "All right. Leave all that all-knowing business. Tell me why you didn't come yesterday. It means you starved yesterday. Right?" Bhagawan asked.
> "I couldn't come. I was lucky earlier. You know that old age disables the body. Even if I have strong determination,

I cannot overcome the natural weaknesses that beset the aged."
"That's true."
"And we did have Bhagawan's darshan. In those days, you sat on the rock near the [Skand] ashram brushing your teeth. From my house near Arunachaleswara temple, I could have your darshan everyday. Now you are not to be seen. And I cannot come all the way here everyday!"
Bhagawan laughed this time and said:
"What is the problem? It is easily solved. You want to see me. It can still be done."

Ever since, come rain or shine, Bhagawan sat on the rock and brushed his teeth. The elderly people who benefited from this were many and not this lady alone. Many saw the radiant face of Bhagawan from afar. Sitting on the rock, he gave them what they wanted. And there was no need for the devotees, to cite a metaphor from my mentor Sri Ram, "to brush their teeth with the neem twig of Vedanta" to have the glorious darshan of Bhagawan.

Love, longing and surrender were enough for Bhagawan to sit rock-like and receive whoever came with a grace and a concern rare in the spiritual sagas of humanity. Distance is itself distanced.

18

Bhagawan: The Master Storyteller

Saints and sages are fond of telling stories. One could call the tales story-shaped spirituality. Many reasons can be cited for this tendency to tell stories. The basic one is to avoid abstractions, or rather to make abstract ideas concrete. By giving an important teaching, flesh and blood through characters and incidents, the idea becomes humanised though not in the sense humanists use it, but in a sense the 'lessons' are given human contexts. The aspirant (of whatever path) thus empathises and may draw the necessary lesson.

For children, "Once upon a time ..." is enough to make them forget all time. Most of us are children in the field of the inner quest, perhaps children who, having lost their innocence, want to recapture and re-live it. Hence the sages' strategy of telling stories.

Ramana Maharshi is very much one of these superb entrancing storytellers. His own life is a story: almost incredible in its beginnings, marvelous in its unobtrusive manifestation and aweinspiring in its temporal close. His uniquely creative mind intoxicated everyone with his narratives.

Stories are usually a blending of fact and fiction. But when an Incarnate Divine Being tells them, the telling is different. The tenets embodied in such stories are truths; neither mere facts nor vacuous fantasies; they reflect and almost always evoke deep emotions. While ordinary narrators "Tell", sages "Show", registering the essence of their stories in their own consciousness. Maharshi could not, we have been told, tell his stories without himself getting deeply moved. For instance, Bhagawan has been depicted thus: "Describing Gautama's joy at Godess Parvati's coming to his Ashram, it is said he could not go on, for tears filled his eyes and emotion choked his voice."

Bhagawan understood the oddity of an imperturbable *Jnani* such as himself becoming emotional. He explained: "I don't know how people who perform Hari Katha and who explain such passages to audiences manage to do it without breaking down before starting their work." Telling stories without the teller breaking down! The situation seems odd, especially when a person like Bhagawan himself is subject to emotions.

Here is the difference, perhaps, between Bhagawan telling a story and a Bhagavathar telling it. When Sri Nagamma said that telling the story of Tara Vilasam he "appears to have transformed himself into Tara," Bhagawan was said to have remarked, "what to do? I identify myself with whosoever is before me; I have no separate identity. I am universal." In short, the ego is left intact in an ordinary narrator; of course, it responds but impersonally, with an ephemeral emotion evoked by the story. Once the context is removed, the emotion dries up. In a Jnani the sensibility of emotion needs neither context nor pretext. That susceptibility is, simply, consciousness that is all-pervasive and free from the slightest taint of ego.

This leads us to uncover another dimension of this fascinating subject of sages telling stories. Only sages can tell a story with total emotional engagement yet remain detached. That is, the sage remains insulated from the temporal nature in which all stories are formed. A Jnani is detached but delightedly so; his/her detachment comes from delight in the fact that in the cosmic system all our responses (emotional or cerebral) are responses to the Drama of life, to the Lila, the play of the Lord or Nature (whichever one prefers). Sympathetic Uninvolvement would, perhaps, describe this.

There are many contexts in Bhagawan's own story, which illustrate this glorious detachment, superhuman, as it appears to us, in its endurance. Take the most significant, the 'last' phase of Maharshi's life. The narrative of this phase harrows us with fear and wonder. How could or why should Bhagawan suffer? With his adamantine *Samkalpa*, it is, we believe, possible to put an end to suffering in no time. Prarabdha he does not have; in his life there is nothing to explain why he should suffer as he did. Why did he go through this? On the physical level, Bhagawan's experience of suffering is, for us, even in imagination, intolerable to contemplate. Tears well up, the heart is, as it were, rent asunder and we inwardly cry in anguish: 'We can't bear to tolerate this! How can this kind of thing befall one like Bhagawan?'

Thus, we take a leap from the truths of the stories he tells (even now, and even in English, His Narrating Voice comes through!) to His Own Story which is Truth sustaining all those truths. If his own life-story is read as a narrative, then it is parallel to the delight we get from the other stories he told, which we quite often forget, are extensions, live centres of consciousness, of his own life-story.

He told a story as, using today's jargon, an Intertext, the text being his life. Quite often we miss this text. Thus, our responses to His suffering can be exquisitely moving, deeply felt. Yet, in this case, there is hardly any line we can draw between the devotees who knew the essential Bhagawan and the medical doctors who tried all methods to cure his body. That is, the overpowering emotion of the devotees, at seeing Bhagawan suffer, required the further thrust that could transmute their suffering into Jnana.

The stories Bhagawan told and the stories abounding in his own life are a testing ground for awareness in all its complexity. For instance, take the seemingly simple story of Bhagawan gently correcting an attendant who sought to prevent an American lady from stretching out her stiff legs towards him since doing so was 'disrespectful to Bhagawan.' "It is disrespectful, is it?" said Bhagawan, "then it is equally disrespectful for me to stretch my legs towards them. What you say applies to me as well," said Bhagawan and promptly sat cross-legged in spite of rheumatism causing him considerable pain.

The devotee did not see beyond the etiquette of how to sit in the presence of a sage. But Bhagawan linked the incident to the classic story of Avvaiyar who, when asked to, correctly responded: "Tell me on which side *Isvara* is not present. Shall I turn this side?"[5] This story happened in the presence of Siva who thus taught Parvati that He is present everywhere. So too Bhagawan transfigured time and space declaring, "it is similar to that when people are asked not to stretch their legs towards Swami. Where is He not present?" Yes, indeed: Where is Bhagawan not present? In the story, outside the story. In his story and in the stories of all of us. But to link His story with ours is the greatest truth evident in the stories he told. And if all of us are potential *Jnanis*, our stories can be viewed as negatives waiting to be processed into positives, in which their full potential will be manifested. Bhagawan is, in this sense, while gentle, explosively persuasive and, above all, irresistible—also so positive.

www.ingramcontent.com/pod-product-compliance
Lightning Source LLC
Chambersburg PA
CBHW060332050426
42449CB00011B/2730